Success in AQA
Language
&Literature

Steven Croft
Robert Myers

OXFORD
UNIVERSITY PRESS

OXFORD

UNIVERSITY PRESS

Great Clarendon Street, Oxford OX2 6DP

Oxford University Press is a department of the University of Oxford.
It furthers the University's objective of excellence in research, scholarship,
and education by publishing worldwide in

Oxford New York

Athens Auckland Bangkok Bogotá Buenos Aires Calcutta Cape Town
Chennai Dar es Salaam Delhi Florence Hong Kong Istanbul Karachi
Kuala Lumpur Madrid Melbourne Mexico City Mumbai Nairobi
Paris São Paulo Shanghai Singapore Taipei Tokyo Toronto Warsaw

with associated companies in
Berlin Ibadan

Oxford is a registered trade mark of Oxford University Press
in the UK and in certain other countries

A CIP catalogue record for this book is available from the British Library

ISBN 0 19 831479 5

Designed by Mike Brain Graphic Design Limited, Oxford

Typeset by AFS Image Setters Ltd, Glasgow

Printed in Great Britain by Alden Press Ltd, Oxford

Orders and enquiries to Customer Services:
Tel: 01536 741068   Fax: 01536 454519

Contents

Acknowledgements

The authors and publisher are grateful for permission to reprint the following copyright material:

The Assessment and Qualifications Alliance (AQA): extract in 'Practice Paper 1' from *AEB English Language Paper* 1 (Summer, 1999) reprinted by permission of the AQA.

Iain Banks: extracts from *The Wasp Factory* (Abacus), and from *Complicity* (Abacus); both reprinted by permission of Little Brown and Company (UK).

Pat Barker: extract from *The Ghost Road* (Viking, 1995) copyright © Pat Barker 1995, reprinted by permission of Penguin Books Ltd.

Alan Bennett: extract from *Talking Heads 2* (BBC Worldwide Limited, 1998), copyright © Alan Bennett 1998, reprinted by permission of the publisher.

The Big Issue: Vendor's Voice, 'The Killing Fields' from *The Big Issue*, October 1999, reprinted by permission of the publisher.

Bill Bryson: extract from *Notes From a Small Country* (Doubleday, a division of Transworld Publishers, 1995), copyright © Bill Bryson 1995; extract from *Notes From a Big Country* (Doubleday, a division of Transworld Publishers, 1998), copyright © Bill Bryson 1998; both reprinted by permission Transworld Publishers Ltd. All rights reserved.

Ronald Carter and Michael McCarthy: extract from *Exploring Spoken English* (Cambridge University Press, 1997), reprinted by permission of the publisher.

Pauline Cartledge: 'Like Mother Like Son' first published in *The Daily Telegraph*, 3.5.97, reprinted by permission of The Telegraph Group.

Jonathan Coe: extract from *House of Sleep* (Viking, 1997), copyright © Jonathan Coe 1997, reprinted by permission of Penguin Books Ltd and Peake Associates.

Countryside Alliance Campaign for Hunting: extract from *Hunting in the 21st Century* (1999) reprinted by permission.

Carol Ann Duffy: 'Havisham' from *Mean Time* (Anvil Press Poetry Ltd, 1993) reprinted by permission of the publisher.

Gerald Durrell: extract from *My Family and Other Animals* (Penguin Books, 1956), copyright © Gerald Durrell 1956, reprinted by permission of Curtis Brown Ltd, London, on behalf of the Estate of Gerald Durrell.

Adam Edwards: 'Brand on the Run' first published in *Virgin In-flight*, August 1999, reprinted by permission of Virgin Atlantic Airways.

David Guterson: extract from *Snow Falling on Cedars* (Bloomsbury, 1995), copyright © David Guterson 1994, reprinted by permission of Sheil Land Associates Ltd on behalf of the author.

Goddard, Shuttleworth and Keen: extract from *The Advanced Level English Language Starter Pack* (Framework Press) reprinted by permission of Heinemann Educational Publishers, a division of Reed Educational & Professional Publishing Ltd.

Christopher Hirst: 'Review: The Code Book' first published in *The Independent Magazine*, 1.7.00, reprinted by permission of Independent Newspapers (UK) Ltd.

Arthur Hughes and Peter Trudgill: extracts from *English Accents and Dialects* (Arnold Publishers, 1996), reprinted by permission of the publisher.

Colin Irwin: extract from 'Review of the Voice of the People', copyright © Colin Irwin 1999 from *Folk Roots* Magazine (Jan/Feb 99, issue 187/188), reprinted by permission of the author.

Peter Kane: 'Great, Britain' first published in *Q Magazine*, January 1999, reprinted by permission of EMAP Metro.

John Kelly: 'Teen Talk's All Greek to Adults' first published in the *Daily Express*, 16.5.98, reprinted by permission of Express Newspapers.

Eric Lomax: extract from *The Railway Man* (Jonathan Cape, 1995), reprinted by permission of The Random House Group.

Ian McEwan: extract from *The Child in Time* (Jonathan Cape, 1987), copyright © Ian McEwan 1987, reprinted by permission of the author c/o Rogers Coleridge & White Ltd, 20 Powis Mews, London W11 1JN.

Blake Morrison: extract from *As If* (Granta), reprinted by permission of PFD on behalf of Blake Morrison.

Gillian Moseley: 'First Person' first published in *Scotland on Sunday*, 25.8.96, reprinted by permission of the publisher.

Grace Nichols: 'Be a Butterfly' from *The Fat Black Woman's Poems* (Virago Press, 1984), reprinted by permission of Little Brown and Company (UK).

Jeremy Paxman: extract from *The English* (Michael Joseph Ltd), reprinted by permission of David Higham Associates Ltd.

Jonathon Petre: 'Schoolchildren Pocket Money up to £25 a Week' first published in *The Sunday Telegraph*, 16.11.97, reprinted by permission of The Telegraph Group.

E. Annie Proulx: extract from *The Shipping News* (Fourth Estate, 1993), reprinted by permission of HarperCollins Publishers.

Karl Shapiro: 'The Dirty Word' from *Collected Poems 1940–1978* (Wieser & Wieser, New York, 1978), © Karl Shapiro 1978, reprinted by permission of the publisher.

Earl Spencer: extract from his address at the funeral of Diana, Princess of Wales, reprinted by permission of Earl Spencer.

Katherine Whitehorn: 'A Lot, That's What's in a Name', © The Observer 1984, first published in *The Observer* 30.10.94, reprinted by permission of Guardian Newspapers Ltd.

John Windsor: 'Gobsmacked by Shrimping Dweebs' first published in *The Independent*, 10.9.94, reprinted by permission of Independent Newspapers (UK) Ltd.

The publisher would like to thank the following for permission to reproduce photographs: Rex Features (pages 8, 68, 130, 142), National Portrait Gallery (page 30), Little Brown/Craig Stennett (page 56), Royal Shakespeare Company/D. Cooper (pages 87 and 110). We are also grateful to the following students for allowing us to use their responses as examples: Ruth Chester, Sandra Haigh, and Amy Shepherd. Any example answers to examination questions or hints on answers used in this book are the sole responsibility of the authors and have not been provided or approved by the examining boards.

Although we have tried to trace and contact copyright holders before publication, in some cases this has not been possible. If contacted we will be pleased to rectify any errors or omissions at the earliest opportunity.

Paul Ableman: extract from *Emily and Heathcliff* (Methuen Playscripts).

Simon Armitage: 'Very Simply Topping up the Brake Fluid' from *The New Poetry* edited by Hulse, Kennedy and Morley (Bloodaxe); 'A Meteorite' and 'Goalkeeper with a Cigarette' from *The Dead Sea Poems* (Faber & Faber).

Nik Berg: 'Top Speed' first published in *Maxim*, March 2000

David Hare: extract from 'Murmuring Judges' (Faber & Faber).

J. C. Heritage & D. R. Watson: extract from 'Formulations as Conversational Objects' from *Everyday Language* edited by G. Psathas.

Ian Hislop: 'You Want Peace . . .' first published in *The Sunday Telegraph*, 22.6.97.

Sebastian Junger: extract from *The Perfect Storm* (Fourth Estate).

David Langford: extract from *Analysing Talk* (Methuen, 1994).

Toni Morrison: extract from *Beloved* (Chatto & Windus, 1987).

NSPCC: 'What's it Like to be Neglected?' from *The Forgotten Child* (NSPCC, 1986).

Sylvia Plath: extract from *The Bell Jar* (Faber & Faber).

Jonathan Raban: extract from *Coasting* (Picador).

Arthur Smith: 'Swearing Blind' first published in *The Big Issue*, 4.1.94.

Brian Stone: extract from *The Poetry of Keats*.

B. Torode: extract from 'Negotiating Advice' from *The Discourse of Negotiation* edited by A. Firth (1995).

Introduction

This book is designed to help you through your studies at AS and A2 Level, and to help you achieve success in the examinations set by AQA Specification A for English Language and Literature. The tasks and assignments that accompany the wide variety of texts in this book require you to have studied each section of the course previously. We recommend that you do this with the guidance given in our book *Exploring Language and Literature*, which details all the subject content required for this course of study. Each of the chapters in this text parallels the chapters in *Exploring Language and Literature*, so you should be able to cross-reference the content with ease.

The texts and extracts printed here are designed to give you the best possible practice for those you will be faced with in the examination room. You should complete each of the activities, and work carefully through the practice assignments at the end of each chapter.

Sample student answers throughout the book give you a flavour of the kinds of essays it is possible to write under timed conditions. They are in no way perfect or model answers, and they should simply be viewed as one possible route through a question.

We hope that you find the texts, activities and assignments in this book stimulating and challenging, as well as being useful for examination preparation in general. If you complete all the activities, you will be excellently prepared for success in your language and literature studies.

1 Language Production

Introduction

The first unit you will be faced with in your Language & Literature examinations, either in January or June, is the Language Production unit. This is intended as a bridge or stepping-stone between the kinds of tasks you have been used to doing at GCSE and the more demanding types of assignment you will meet in the A2 part of this course.

Since it is likely that this unit will form the basis of your AS studies, as well as being the first unit you tackle, this section of the book gives you a wide variety of texts to use as springboards for your own language production, tasks to accompany each text, and possible areas for you to explore in your commentaries. It will also provide you with an introduction to different styles of writing, giving you a very valuable introduction to the diversity of texts you may come across in your English course.

The more experience you have of looking at other people's writing and practising your own writing skills, the more you will achieve in dealing with the questions in this module.

All of the following stimulus texts are 'real'; they have been taken from printed material that was written for a specific audience with an explicit purpose in mind. The tasks you will be set will always aim to be as realistic as possible, despite the fact that you are writing within an examination context, which is a false and manufactured situation. You will therefore gain practice in the types of production task you may face on a day-to-day basis, as well as being fully prepared for an examination.

The texts and tasks

Each of the texts in this chapter has been selected because it affords a number of opportunities. First, the texts are intrinsically interesting because of their subject matter, their form, the way they use language and so on. Secondly, they are all viable springboard texts for use in this examination and they provide excellent practice in writing for different situations and audiences. Remember that a springboard text is a stimulus for your own writing; this unit is not concerned with recasting work, which appears in Unit 5.

The tasks are divided into separate parts: the first part draws your attention to some of the issues that make each text interesting, and concentrates on the ways each writer uses language for a particular purpose. The second part is the production assignment, reflecting the type of task you are likely to be set in the examination.

Text 1

The following text was written by the comedian Arthur Smith, who is often to be seen on television programmes such as *Whose Line Is It Anyway?* and *They Think It's All Over.* He wrote this article for publication in *The Big Issue.*

SWEARING BLIND

I like swearing. I swear at home, at parties, on stage, on the street, on the phone. I swear when I am angry, but also when I'm happy and, indeed, when I have no strong feelings at all. I even swear in articles for *The Big Issue* – but not yet.

Naturally enough this offends some people. A common complaint is that swearing 'shows your lack of vocabulary'. This is easy for me to refute, since, without looking them up, I know the meaning of nearly all these words: nugatory, jejune, serendipity and anthropomorphic. Besides, the people who make this sterile remark are the ones who describe everything as 'nice'.

When I swear on stage I am told it is just an easy way to get a laugh. There is truth in this. A weak punch-line can definitely be perked up by the judicious insertion of an oath, just as a dull evening can be enlivened by a brace of tequila slammers. But a piss-poor act remains piss-poor however often the performer says 'piss', and 14 slammers don't necessarily guarantee a great night out.

These musings are prompted by a letter I received from a TV director yesterday. I am doing five minutes of old gags on a regional TV show, and the letter contains strictures on what is, and is not, acceptable.

I shan't put any swearwords in my routine on the programme, not because it is pathetic and puerile, but because I've already done it: I am responsible for the foulest outpouring of profanity ever issued on a British TV programme. Let me explain.

I was in an episode of *Red Dwarf* which took place on a planet where time ran in reverse. The lines I had to deliver were to be transmitted backwards, and would therefore appear in that soup of wheeps and sucks that is backwards talk. I put it to the writers Rob Grant and Doug Naylor that I might as well come on and swear outrageously and that this would be a splendid in-joke for everyone concerned. Rob and Doug can be as puerile and pathetic as the next schoolboy and they gleefully agreed. I duly used every swear word I know as verb, adjective, noun and again in the plural for good measure. The studio audience looked very shocked. I forgot about it until two years later when a man stopped me in the street and remarked slyly that he could run his video backwards and that he had seen *Red Dwarf.* We shared a conspiratorial snigger.

Nevertheless I am pleased I can't swear on TV and I am always happy when people get upset by my language. If they didn't it would be no fun. If a word loses its power to shock and offend then it isn't a swear word any more. And who wants a language with no fucking swear words?

Analytical tasks

1 What is the purpose of Arthur Smith's article?

2 How does he ensure that his article hits the right note with his audience?

3 In what ways does he use humour to reinforce his arguments in this text?

4 Arthur Smith makes reference to particular events that have happened to him. Why does he do this, and how does this help to support the point of his article?

Points of linguistic interest

◆ the use of demotic, or street, language
◆ his employment of the first person pronominative form
◆ the variety of simple, compound and complex sentences
◆ the use of *The Big Issue* to promote his views.

Assignment

Having read Arthur Smith's article in *The Big Issue*, you are moved to respond to it because of the issues it discusses. Write a letter to the magazine in which you air your views, arguing your points logically and cogently.

Next, write a brief commentary in which you reflect on the ways you used language to endorse the views you put forward in your letter.

Text 2

This piece of writing was produced for a competition run by *The Daily Telegraph*. Readers were invited to write a mini-saga – a story of not more than 50 words. The winning entry from the 1997 competition was penned by Pauline Cartledge. She uses letters (the epistolary form) to construct her mini-saga.

LIKE MOTHER, LIKE SON

1955

Dear Mummy,

I hate this boarding school. Food awful, prefects bully me. Please take me home.

Love, David.

Dear David,

Nonsense! Chin up.

Mother.

1997

Dear David,

I hate this Home. Food awful, nurses treat me like a child. Fetch me immediately.

Mother.

Dear Mother,

Nonsense! Chin up.

David

Analytical tasks

1 How does Pauline Cartledge construct a voice for each of the characters in this mini-saga?

2 In what ways does the use of letters help her overall purpose?

Points of linguistic interest

◆ the use of two very different voices to reflect the characters' language
◆ the importance of the context of each letter
◆ the 'simplicity' of each communication and the 'complexity' of its message
◆ the use of idiom.

Assignment

Choose either of the characters in this text, and write two or three diary entries for your chosen character at the time (*either* 1955 *or* 1997) they received or sent their letters. You should aim to write about 500 words in total.

In a brief commentary, show how you have established the voice of your character through your specific linguistic choices.

Text 3

The following article appeared in *The Sunday Telegraph* in November 1997; the amounts of pocket money it discusses may now seem ungenerous in the light of inflation, but the issues it raises remain pertinent.

SCHOOLCHILDREN POCKET UP TO £25 A WEEK

Children have never had it so good: the average secondary school pupil is pocketing a weekly income of £17, with 16-year-olds raking in £25, a new study has found.

The report, by the National Foundation for Educational Research, has surprised educationalists, who said the 'colossal' size of teenage incomes reflected a 'mercenary' culture. But financial experts said it showed an urgent need to teach children about money.

The survey of 11- to 16-year-olds at state and independent secondary schools found that the average weekly income for boys is £17.74, made up of pocket money supplemented by earnings from chores at home and part-time jobs. Significantly, the figure dropped to £15.06 for girls.

Older children do substantially better than younger ones, with average weekly income rising from £7.51 for 11-year-olds to £24.77 for 16-year-olds, the study says. About three-quarters of pupils are paid for work done around the house, and a similar proportion earn extra money from jobs elsewhere. Nearly three in ten said they saved every week, with almost the same number saying they did so regularly.

While items like cinema tickets, magazines and snacks were popular among children, parents were still left picking up some of the biggest bills for luxuries such as computer games and holidays.

The study, which is to be unveiled at a London conference tomorrow by Government curriculum advisers and the NatWest bank, shows that boys receive an average of £5.15 pocket money, £3.46 from chores and £8.73 from part-time work. The figures for girls were £4.93, £2.26 and £7.60 respectively. Each gets a small amount from other sources.

While there have been no comparable surveys of the 11 to 16 age group in the past, other surveys show that weekly pocket money for children aged five to 16 averaged £2.33 this year, compared with £1.16 a decade ago. The figures show that pocket money has easily outstripped the headline rate of inflation – which went up by 46 per cent over the same period – rising by 54 per cent in real, after-inflation terms.

The latest sign of affluence among children comes amid growing concern about the amounts of money young people are spending on alcohol, cigarettes and lottery scratch cards.

Yesterday educationalists warned that too much money could damage children's understanding of its true value.

Nick Seaton, spokesman for the Real Education group, said: 'It is a colossal amount of money and far beyond the needs of teenagers. In these circumstances, parents and teachers should not be surprised that young people have no difficulty getting alcohol, tobacco and, in some cases, drugs. It shows a mercenary attitude among the young. I am all for enterprise, but this is giving youngsters the impression that money is very easy to get in real life.'

Analytical tasks

1 What is the purpose of a piece of writing such as this?

2 Who is the target audience?

3 How does this piece of writing use facts, figures and opinion to further its purpose?

Points of linguistic interest

◆ the use of adverbs
◆ how facts and figures are used
◆ the semantic field of money and finance.

Assignment

You have been asked, as a student, to give your views on the perception that young people 'have never had it so good'.

Your local newspaper will print your views in a section devoted to issues concerning young people. Your article should be concise and to the point, as there is space for only about 400 words.

In a textual commentary, analyse one or two examples of the ways in which you have used language in your article to further your argument, as well as giving a general overview of what you wanted to achieve in your writing.

Text 4

This text was used by the NSPCC in 1986 to raise awareness about children suffering from neglect in this country. It is taken from *The Forgotten Child*.

WHAT'S IT LIKE TO BE NEGLECTED?

Try and imagine what it feels like to be neglected.

Pretend you're five years old. Your mum wakes you at eight to go to school. But you're still tired. You didn't get to bed until eleven – about the same time as your mum and dad. And you didn't sleep very well. Your bedroom's cold and there's only one thin blanket on your bed. You get up and put on the clothes you had on yesterday. They're dirty – you spilt milk down your shirt the day before yesterday. But that's nothing unusual. You don't wash. No one tells you to and, anyway, it's cold in the bathroom. Your mother's gone back to bed and your father's already left for work so you go into the kitchen to get your own breakfast. All you can find is biscuits – so you eat one. You don't want to finish them off in case your mum and dad get angry.

You leave for school. It's cold but you haven't got a warm anorak – just a thin plastic mac. The last anorak you had is much too small for you now.

School wasn't much fun today – and your teacher was cross because you arrived late. None of your classmates wanted to sit next to you and you heard them whispering that you were smelly. At play-time, no one wanted to play with you.

At three o'clock, you began to walk home on your own. Most of the other children of your age were met by one of their parents. You thought how nice it would be if your mother came to meet you. But she never does any more.

Analytical tasks

1 What does the writer do to stimulate an emotional reaction to this piece of writing?

2 Try switching the story into the third-person narrative form. What is the effect of this change?

Points of linguistic interest

◆ the use of the second-person pronominative form
◆ the use of simple lexis
◆ the narrative structure of the piece.

Assignment

Using this piece of writing as the basis for your own work, write a scene between the head teacher and this child, where the head teacher asks the child why no one meets him or her after school any more. You are free to choose any genre you wish.

In a commentary, use a couple of well-chosen examples from your piece of writing to show how you have used language to capture the voice of each of the characters in your work.

Text 5

The article below appeared in a Virgin Airlines in-flight magazine in August 1999. In the article, the writer extols the virtues of Virgin products and endorses the entrepreneurship of Virgin's boss, Richard Branson.

BRAND ON THE RUN

Let's be candid: how many T-shirts and baseball hats can one man wear? We know that if Richard Branson could wear all the Virgin sweatshirts and hats on this plane, while playing patience with all the Virgin playing cards, and be photographed doing it, he would love it.

We know he would he happy to paint not just his pinkie but all of his fingers and toes with bottles and bottles of Virgin Vie nail varnish, pausing only to curl up with as many Virgin Biggles Bears as is humanly possible, if it meant just one more picture. To wake him, a million Virgin alarm clocks could ring all together, louder than Big Ben, and the man would be proud.

You can even see him with Virgin wristwatches by the score running up his arm, Virgin funwatches and dual time watches hanging from inside his coat (well, actually a Virgin Fleece) like a 1950s cartoon smuggler.

As a one-man publicity machine he has no equal. Yet despite his greatest efforts, somebody else still has to help him wear the Virgin logo.

The Virgin logo represents a brand rather than a product. It does not imply that you do your shopping at the local Supersaver, or that you eat at the ubiquitous McBurger takeaway. It is not a logo that suggests you went on a Saga holiday nor one that implies you have been trailing behind your parents in shades, pretending you are not with them. You weren't on holiday with Stupid, nor was your only present a lousy T-shirt.

Instead, the logo is a badge of honour. The fashionable wear the Virgin logo. It implies independence and adventure, standing for youth and confidence. Furthermore, it looks good, and in the end, that is what matters.

Nobody minds wearing the Levi's logo on the back of their jeans because it is perfectly cool and the product is great. So too are Rayban sunglasses, Cartier and Chanel, and even Marlboro cigarettes. But logos aren't just for companies, they also represent international brand identification. Countries have used logos for centuries, only they called them flags back then. The Stars and Stripes, the Rising Sun and the Union Jack need no words to tell you what they represent.

So you must forgive Richard his love of Virgin. He simply wants to fly his flag proudly. And despite his best efforts he cannot be everywhere at the same time. He needs help. To subvert Uncle Sam and Lord Kitchener's exhortation: 'This Company Needs You'. And, anyway, the stuff is pretty good.

Richard Branson sporting the Virgin logo

Analytical tasks

1 In what ways, and to what effect, does the writer use positive language in this article?

2 What use of rhetorical and persuasive devices does the writer use? Why?

Points of linguistic interest

◆ comparison and parallelism
◆ the use of proper nouns and lists
◆ the address to the reader
◆ the use of colloquialisms and informality.

Assignment

As part of a national competition being run by *The Sunday Times*, you have been asked to endorse a particular product or brand of your choice, by writing a magazine article in a lively and original way. The winner will be printed in the Review section of the paper, and the entry should be no more than 450 words.

In a textual commentary, focus on how you have used language and any particular devices in order to endorse your chosen product. You should also briefly mention why you chose that particular product or brand.

Questions with two or more texts as stimulus

You may be faced with two or more texts as part of your stimulus material; this will be because they are short, contain a variety of ideas and can give you more material to draw from. It may also be appropriate to give you a variety of texts which you can skim through, selecting one as your preferred springboard.

Text 6

This text is from Blake Morrison's reflections on the Jamie Bulger trial, entitled *As If*. Here he describes the day the trial opened in Preston.

November 1, bitter dawn-light, and I stand in a square in Preston, waiting for a transit van. Round the corner, in the covered Victorian market, traders are setting up their stalls: toys, children's clothes, discarded kitchenware, cheap videos, empty golf bags, local maps in dusty frames – but no one yet to buy. An encampment of outside broadcast vans, here for a snooker tournament, sprawls in the other direction – no signs of life there, either. But in the gloom of this cobbled square, under a sky smudged like newsprint, up from the monument to the massacred mill-workers, the first grey souls are flitting through.

Text 7

The following is the opening to Sebastian Junger's biographical account of how a fishing boat was lost at sea ; the book is called *The Perfect Storm*.

A soft fall rain slips down through the trees and the smell of ocean is so strong that it can almost be licked off the air. Trucks rumble along Rogers Street and men in t-shirts stained with fishblood shout to each other from the decks of boats. Beneath them the ocean swells up against the black pilings and sucks back down to the barnacles. Beer cans and old pieces of styrofoam rise and fall and pools of spilled diesel fuel undulate like huge iridescent jellyfish. The boats rock and creak against their ropes and seagulls complain and hunker down and complain some more. Across Rogers Street and around the back of the Crow's Nest Inn, through the door and up the cement stairs, down the carpeted hallway and into one of the doors on the left, stretched out on a double bed in room #27 with a sheet pulled over him, Bobby Shatford lies asleep.

He's got one black eye. There are beer cans and food wrappers scattered around the room and a duffel bag on the floor with t-shirts and flannel shirts and blue jeans spilling out.

Analytical tasks

1   How does each of the writers establish a sense of atmosphere through the language that they use?

2   How is the narrative viewpoint used in each piece?

Points of linguistic interest

◆   description and adjectival use
◆   the mood of each piece
◆   the use of pathetic fallacy and images.

Assignment

You have been asked to write, as part of your English course, an extended piece of autobiographical writing, where you can practise using first-person narrative.

As an opening to your autobiography, you have decided to set the mood for the whole piece by concentrating on one particular event. Write this opening section in about 300–400 words. Simply set the scene; you do *not* need to go into the narrative details of your chosen incident.

> In a commentary, reflect on how you created your mood by analysing one or two carefully chosen parts of your writing, explaining how they contribute to the overall effect.

Text 8

This review of a book appeared in *The Independent* newspaper.

THE CODE BOOK

By Simon Singh
(Fourth Estate, £7.99, 402pp)

It is hard to imagine a more enthralling book which also contains large chunks that will be baffling to readers. This does not merely apply to the 13-page Cipher Challenge – an encrypted message which will earn £10000 for the solver (so far, no one's cracked it).

The key to the readability of Singh's book is the tug of war between code inventors and code crackers. Users have to believe that their codes are uncrackable, otherwise they wouldn't use them. The execution of Mary, Queen of Scots resulted from her coded messages about the assassination of Elizabeth I, which were cracked by Walsingham's cipher secretary. Germany couldn't conceive that messages garbled by its Enigma machines could be penetrated. Yet the code was rapidly cracked, first by the Poles, then by Alan Turing's team at Bletchley. Some readers may be fogged by fine detail, but the mists clear when the book turns to American wartime codes which relied on the Navajo language ('Britain' was 'bounded by water').

Even Singh has to curb his passion for explanation when faced by modern computer codes. We can acquire these ciphers ourselves via e-mail. According to Singh, a new development called quantum cryptography is 'an unbreakable system of encryption'. However, it is 400 years too late for Mary, Queen of Scots.

Text 9

This review for a car-cum-bike appeared in *Maxim* magazine.

TOP SPEED

The Ariel Atom

Time was when you knew where you were. A car was a car and a bike was a bike. Men were men and women weren't. But now the boundaries have been blurred as any visit to the 'chicks with dicks' website will tell you. And when it comes to wheels, things don't get any less bizarre.

The Ariel Atom is the car that thinks it's a motorbike. It may have four wheels on the ground and one in your hands, but that's the extent of the creature comforts.

There are no doors, no windscreen, no roof and definitely no heater or CD player. In winter you'll have to wear your warmest skiwear and you'll need a crash helmet to avoid a facial bug-blasting.

Some might say that this gives you the worst of both worlds – none of the comfort of a car with none of the convenience of a motorbike. But they should stick to their cosy Corsas as they've completely missed the point of this vehicle. The Atom is designed to be the most pure, raw driver's car ever made. It's the closest thing to a road-legal racer.

Its steel-tube chassis is built for stiffness and weight-saving (hence no body panels), the suspension uses the same style of double-wishbones and in-board dampers that you'll find in Formula One. The engine, slung behind the driver for ideal handling, musters 125bhp from a 1.8-litre engine, but versions with over 200 bhp will also be available. Bear in mind that the Atom weighs just over 500 kg and you're looking at Porsche-pasting performance.

Although it is road-legal, the Atom's natural habitat is the track, where you can enjoy it to the full without appearing on *Police Stop!* Strapped into the moulded plastic bucket-seat by a four-point race harness and with the quick-release steering wheel snapped into place, it's like waiting on the grid at Silverstone. Press the starter button (there's no ignition key) and the engine bursts into life. You'll be doing 60 in the time it takes to say, 'Jeeeeesus.' There's tons of grip if you want it, but the car has also been set up for high-speed hi-jinks and can be slid through corners in a rallying sideways fashion as well.

A basic track car costs just £14,500, while a road racer is no more than £19,000. OK, so you might need to sell both your bike and car to get one, but on this occasion it could just be worth it.

Text 10

This review for a CD appeared in a magazine that focuses on traditional roots music, called *The Living Tradition*.

GRAND HOTEL

Mad Pudding
Fellside FECD149

Here, exclusively for Living Tradition readers, is the authentic recipe for one of the finest dishes to come out of Canada: Mad Pudding.

For the base: take the traditional music of these islands, remove to the New World and allow to mix and mature in the chiller for a century or two. Sprinkle with essence of Brazil, Persia and France.

For the filling: carefully build layer upon sumptuous layer of guitar, bass, drums, accordion, fiddle, whistle and piano. Add some fine contemporary writing, and when the dish is full season with a dash of Leonard Cohen, a pinch of Brahms, and a soupçon of Copeland. Wrap in the Mason's apron and leave to set.

Western Canadian cuisine is possibly less familiar to the British palate than the popular dishes of Cape Breton, but is surely in no way inferior. This fine repast is best served alfresco, accompanied by copious quantities of draught beer, shared with friends at festivals. However, thanks to Fellside, it is now available for home consumption at your own convenience. Gourmets amongst you may possibly consider that the latter version is ever so slightly overcooked and underspiced in comparison, but you will dine on nothing finer this year.

Health fact: due to Mad Pudding having an innate ability to bring about dancing amongst those partaking of it, it is unique in the world of puddings in that the more you sample it the more weight you will lose! Enjoy!

Analytical tasks

1   What techniques does each writer use to convey his or her feelings about the product being reviewed?

2   How do the writers use value-laden vocabulary to help their argument?

Points of linguistic interest

◆   the way facts are conveyed
◆   adjectival use
◆   use of recognized formats and parallel structures
◆   the use of humour.

Assignment

You have been asked to write a review of **one** of the following for your school or college magazine:

◆   a recently released film
◆   a concert that you attended
◆   a new restaurant that has opened in your town.

In a textual commentary, reflect on the following areas:

◆   the form you chose to use as the structure for your review
◆   how you used language to reflect your attitude and views.

Using literary texts

Whilst the springboard text will always be from a **non-fiction** source, it will be helpful if you also look at literary extracts when you prepare for this unit, since the task you could be given can be of a literary nature. This will also help you to concentrate on purpose and audience as well as preparing you for the synoptic paper, which will always have a literary piece of writing as part of the analytical textual comparison.

Text 11

This is the opening to Sylvia Plath's novel *The Bell Jar.*

It was a queer, sultry summer, the summer they electrocuted the Rosenbergs, and I didn't know what I was doing in New York. I'm stupid about executions. The idea of being electrocuted makes me sick, and that's all there was to read in the papers – goggle-eyed headlines staring up at me on every street corner and the fusty, peanut-smelling mouth of every subway. It had nothing to do with me, but I couldn't help wondering what it would be like, being burned alive all along your nerves.

New York was bad enough. By nine in the morning the fake, country-wet freshness that somehow seeped in overnight evaporated like the tail end of a sweet dream. Mirage-grey at the bottom of their granite canyons, the hot streets wavered in the sun, the car tops sizzled and glittered, and the dry, cindery dust blew into my eyes and down my throat.

I thought it must be the worst thing in the world.

I kept hearing about the Rosenbergs over the radio and at the office till I couldn't get them out of my mind. It was like the first time I saw a cadaver. For weeks afterwards, the cadaver's head – or what there was left of it – floated up behind my eggs and bacon at breakfast and behind the face of Buddy Willard, who was responsible for my seeing it in the first place, and pretty soon I felt as though I were carrying that cadaver's head around with me on a string, like some black, noseless balloon stinking of vinegar.

I knew there was something wrong with me that summer, because all I could think of was the Rosenbergs and how stupid I'd been to buy all those uncomfortable, expensive clothes, hanging limp as fish in my closet, and how all the little successes I'd totted up so happily at college fizzled to nothing outside the slick marble and plate-glass fronts along Madison Avenue.

I was supposed to be having the time of my life. I was supposed to be the envy of thousands of other college girls just like me all over America who wanted nothing more than to be tripping about in those same size seven patent leather shoes I'd bought in Bloomingdale's one lunch hour with a black patent leather belt and black patent leather pocketbook to match.

Analytical tasks

1 In what ways does Plath draw you into her narrative?

2 Which parts of this section are meant to leave an impression? How does she do this?

Points of linguistic interest

◆ use of first-person narrative and the structure of the piece
◆ patterning and recurrence
◆ the 'voice' of the narrator.

Assignment

Using this extract as the basis for your piece of writing, script a dialogue where the narrator tells a friend about the incident where she saw a dead body (cadaver).

In a commentary, focus on how you conveyed the detail of the incident through:

◆ the speech of the narrator
◆ the reaction of the friend.

Text 12

The opening two sections of Jonathon Coe's novel *The House of Sleep* are reproduced below. There are two definite sections here – one a narrative, the other a description.

It was their final quarrel, that much was clear. But although he had been anticipating it for days, perhaps even for weeks, nothing could quell the tide of anger and resentment which now rose up inside him. She had been in the wrong, and had refused to admit it. Every argument he had attempted to put forward, every attempt to be conciliatory and sensible, had been distorted, twisted around and turned back against him. How dare she bring up that perfectly innocent evening he had spent in The Half Moon with Jennifer? How dare she call his gift 'pathetic', and claim that he was looking 'shifty' when he gave it to her? And how *dare* she bring up his mother – his *mother*, of all people – and accuse him of seeing her too often? As if that were some sort of comment on his maturity; on his *masculinity, even* . . .

He stared blindly ahead, unconscious of his surroundings or of his fellow pedestrians. 'Bitch,' he thought to himself, as her words came back to him. And then out loud, through clenched teeth, he shouted, 'BITCH!'

After that, he felt slightly better.

*****

Huge, grey and imposing, Ashdown stood on a headland, some twenty yards from the sheer face of the cliff, where it had stood for more than a hundred years. All day, the gulls wheeled around its spires and tourelles, keening themselves hoarse. All day and all night, the waves threw themselves dementedly against their rocky barricade, sending an endless roar like heavy traffic through the glacial rooms and mazy, echoing corridors of the old house. Even the emptiest parts of Ashdown – and most of it was now empty – were never silent. The most habitable rooms huddled together on the first and second floors, overlooking the sea, and during the day were flooded with chill sunlight. The kitchen, on the ground floor, was long and L-shaped, with a low ceiling; it had only three tiny windows, and was swathed in permanent shadow. Ashdown's bleak, element-defying beauty masked the fact that it was, essentially, unfit for human occupation. Its oldest and nearest neighbours could remember, but scarcely believe, that it had once been a private residence, home to a family of only eight or nine. But two decades ago it had been acquired by the new university, and it now housed about two dozen students: a shifting population, as changeful as the ocean which lay at its feet, stretched towards the horizon, sickly green and heaving with endless disquiet.

Analytical tasks

1 What might be the writer's purpose in starting his novel with two quite different sections?

2 What effect is he seeking to create in each of these sections? How does he do this?

Points of linguistic interest

◆ use of questions
◆ interior monologue and third-person narrative
◆ premodification.

Assignment

You have been asked to continue the story by writing the next two sections of the novel, following this format. For *both* sections, no more than a total of 400–450 words should be used. You can, of course, make one section longer than the other if you wish.

Reflect on your writing in a textual commentary, concentrating on one of the sections you have written, and discussing how you have made particular choices in the way you continued from the novel's opening.

Text 13

This dramatic piece is from Paul Ableman's collection called *Tests*. This is a self-contained playlet for two characters.

1: Once again the lime trees are in blossom.
2: The next train to Putney leaves in twenty years.
1: Once again the turnips are in blossom.
2: My name is Heathcliff.

1: My name is Emily Brontë.

2: My name is Heathcliff.

1: It is a clear, fresh winter morning.

2: The next bus to Torquay leaves in twenty years.

1: Where will you be in twenty years, Heathcliff?

2: My name is Pedro. My home is Catalonia. My heart is my heart.

1: Where will I be in twenty years, Heathcliff?

2: You will be dead in twenty years. It is planned that you will die of tuberculosis.

1: Once again the plum trees are in blossom.

2: The next war begins in twenty years, Emily.

1: Where will you be in twenty years, Heathcliff?

2: In Paris. I mean to live in Paris and have French women.

1: Why?

2: It is the only way for a revolutionary that does not lead to hate.

1: Once more the woods are green.

2: There will be no more revolutions, Emily.

1: The sky is ice, and beyond the sky there is ice. I know there is ice.

2: You are wrong. There is fire.

1: This vernal land once more wears feathers and petals. A dream is a static thing and there's the comfort.

2: There will be no cottages for you, Emily. You will be dead in twenty years, dead as the train leaves for Putney, the bus for Torquay and the race for anger.

1: I am dying of life, Heathcliff.

Analytical tasks

1 What is the impact of the writer's use of non-sequiturs?

2 How does this piece of dialogue use association and reference?

Points of linguistic interest

◆ the use of question and answer
◆ male and female language use
◆ the 'gaps' in the dialogue.

Assignment

Take two lines from this dramatic interchange, working them into a piece of narrative writing of your own in a meaningful way. You may wish to concentrate on one particular part or section of your narrative. In other words, it does not need to be complete.

In a textual commentary, reflect on your use of the two lines in your narrative, and why you chose them in preference to others.

Examination assignment

Question 1

Read the following text carefully. It is a piece of writing intended to highlight the power of metaphor.

Write a story or narrative of your own which helps to explain to a teenage audience the metaphor used in this story. You are free to invent your own characters and setting. Your story is to be printed by your college or school in an anthology of writing, with your accompanying commentary.

THE DIRTY WORD

The dirty word hops in the cage of the mind like the Pondicherry vulture, stomping with its heavy left claw on the sweet meat of the brain and tearing it with its vicious beak, ripping and chopping the flesh. Terrified, the small boy bears the big bird of the dirty word into the house, and, grunting, puffing, carries it up the stairs to his own room in the skull. Bits of black feather cling to his clothes and his hair as he locks the staring creature in the dark closet.

All day the small boy returns to the closet to examine and feed the bird, to caress and kick the bird, that now snaps and flaps its wings savagely whenever the door is opened. How the boy trembles and delights at the sight of the white excrement of the bird! How the bird leaps and rushes against the walls of the skull, trying to escape from the zoo of the vocabulary! How wildly snaps the sweet meat of the brain in its rage.

And the bird outlives the man, being freed at the man's death-funeral by a word from the rabbi.

(But one morning I went upstairs and opened the door and entered the closet and found in the cage of my mind the great bird dead. Softly I wept it and softly removed it and softly buried the body of the bird in the hollyhock garden of the house I lived in twenty years before. And out of the worn black feathers of the wing have I made these pens to write these elegies, for I have outlived the bird, and I have murdered it in my early manhood.)

Question 2

Write a brief commentary on your story, explaining how you interpreted *The Dirty Word* and why you chose your particular narrative.

Student response

<u>Question 1</u>

Looking back on things, there were certain signals, yet they seemed so small and insignificant then. For a little while the quarrels between my Mum and Dad were just the typical arguments that everyone's parents had (or so I tried to convince myself); but it was the day that they spent three hours fighting which concluded with my Dad walking out that the seed of worry and doubt was planted.

I tried to forget about it, even though the words were hateful, but the ideas kept surfacing in my thoughts and dreams again and again.

Broken relationship.

Separation.

Divorce.

That last one was the worst, and from the very moment that I had thought that it might happen to my parents, I knew that until <u>they</u> told me otherwise, I could and would never stop worrying. I didn't know who to turn to; none of my friends would be able to help. Besides, I wasn't sure if I wanted them to know . . . they would think I was a charity case. And how could they give sympathy when they didn't even understand? So I kept my fears to myself, putting them as best as I could to the back of my mind, in the vain hope that if I didn't think about them, they would go away.

People must have known that something was wrong, if not from looking at my parents, from simply observing me. No matter how hard I tried to ignore the problem, it always came back to me. It was like a smell or a stain that you can't get rid of, that follows you around until you become so painfully self-conscious that you want the earth to open up underneath you.

Every day something would trigger my imagination. I would be off in a world of black thoughts where my parents lived separate lives and I was passed blindly between the two. Each day would bring with it different nightmares, diverse and badly edited, uncensored horror films in my mind. Like these films that hold a fascination in their gore, I too would be transfixed, a captive audience in my own brain, until something or someone would jolt me out of my skull's seedy cinema with a comment or an enquiry. To these I would mumble something noncommittal, and try to calm the anarchy in my head.

When it eventually happened, my parent's divorce, that is, I was numb. I think that for so long I had been exposed to the horror movies of my imagination that I had become desensitized to its malice. All it took was

→

the word of one man, an anonymous judge in an anonymous divorce court, to end a marriage and instigate an event which would be with me, part of me, for the rest of my life. Surely, I thought, this will have an influence on everything I do, think, feel or say forever.

As it happened, the divorce, the secret fear that I had harboured for so long before it actually took place, was with me forever, but not in the way that I had thought. Now, several years after, I see that it did shape me, it is part of me, but I am not the gore-spattered victim from the movie that I imagined I would become. Now, I look back on those months and years with something approaching affection. True, those times were painful and I thought they would never end, and that a solution would never be found, but I look at the person that I am today and I wonder if, given other events, I would have ended up the same.

Today, I can remember those days without hurt or fear, I can place them in the span of my life as a time of hardship that I survived, negative, yet distant, from which something good and sound was able to grow.

Question 2

The extract 'The Dirty Word' is most definitely a particularly powerful piece, and is obviously very personal to the author. He does not specify what exactly the 'Dirty Word' is, and this helps greatly in making the piece so very effective. This helped me to choose an appropriate parallel situation without lifting his ideas openly. So I interpreted the 'Dirty Word' as something that my protagonist finds disgusting, fascinating and perhaps even taboo – that is, the theme of divorce and separation and the mental effect it has on the person narrating.

So my interpretation of 'The Dirty Word' as a metaphor for some private and personal fear that the author may have held as a young boy is openly reflected in my use of the ideas of 'his own room', 'in the skull' and 'dark closet'. All of these images demonstrate secrecy, privacy and a need to hide things from others; they are all particularly 'dark', hinting that the 'Dirty Word' is something negative and fearful, not positive. In my piece of writing, I chose to concentrate on the mental torture that the narrator endures, highlighted by use of such phrases as 'a world of black thoughts' and 'a captive audience in my own brain'.

I wanted to use the idea that Shapiro explores so effectively, that is, the confinement that the 'Dirty Word' causes within the narrator's world, with the effect being eventually something malevolent and fearful.

I use an extended metaphor in my piece of work to echo that used by Shapiro in his piece. I talk of the narrator's thoughts having a parallel in cinema. S/he has 'different nightmares, diverse and badly edited' and claims the situation causes 'uncensored horror films in my mind.' The

→

thoughts then become something which s/he cannot leave alone, that 'hold a fascination in their gore' where s/he becomes 'transfixed, a captive audience in my own brain' until reality would 'jolt me out of my skull's seedy cinema'. I think that the use of popular media to mirror the narrator's anguish is something that would readily appeal to the specified teenage audience, who would be able to relate to it in order to understand it.

Shapiro's original metaphor is not completely negative, however. Although the private fear that I interpreted the 'Dirty Word' to be is something that takes over the mind of the boy in the piece – 'How the bird leaps and rushes against the walls of the skull' – the author develops the metaphor in such a way that the ending can be interpreted as quite positive. He tells us that he finds 'the great bird dead', and we are told that he buries it in the 'garden of the house I lived in twenty years before', which can be interpreted as the author telling us that he has now put this private fear in its place deep in the past, where it belongs. This is something that I pick up on and ensure that I leave the reader with an upbeat final line, 'those days . . . I survived . . . from which something good and sound was able to grow'.

Thus the narrator sees the divorce in the family as something that time can heal, and that can be looked upon in hindsight as something character building. This, too, fits in nicely with the original metaphor in 'The Dirty Word', as the reader is aware of a definite passing of time – 'one morning', 'I have outlived the bird', and with this comes the sense of the fear no longer holding any power, just as with a divorce, the majority of the pain and the fear for the young person goes away over time, and eventually, once everything is resolved, the worry holds no control any longer. ◆

Examiner's comments

This is a very successful piece of production work because it:

◆ does not try to deal with the metaphor in a complex manner
◆ will appeal to the audience
◆ shows a clear understanding of the springboard text
◆ uses the first-person narrative form successfully.

The commentary is a superb piece of work since it:

◆ focuses on the task
◆ uses two examples in detail and analyses their effect
◆ is conscious of the limitations of the material
◆ uses the appropriate terminology to aid the analytical points it makes, thus enhancing our understanding of the original work.

2 The Language of Poetry

Introduction

The second unit you will work on is the module entitled 'Poetic Study'. In this module you will focus specifically on the language poets use and how this helps you to explore and illuminate the issues, ideas and feelings that they express in their poems. Because of this focus on linguistic issues it is vital that you know the poetry text you are studying fully, and that you can quickly access the appropriate parts of the text to answer the question.

In order to tackle exam questions it is a good idea to be methodical in your approach to the study of a poem. The following outline is one suggested way of approaching any of the variety of questions that you might be asked.

Framework

◆ Identify what determines poetic language and structure.

Analysis and explanation

◆ Identify, exemplify and explain central features of the poem(s) using contextual and structural frameworks
◆ Describe and contextualize the features of the poem(s), e.g. exploration of ideas, themes, images
◆ Consider meaning and effect
◆ Consider differing levels of analysis.

Evaluation

◆ Briefly consider the text's success with reference to explanatory frameworks.

The specification offers the following advice:

◆ Candidates will be required to comment on specific poems, or sections of longer poems, in their analysis.
◆ Candidates should focus on linguistic matters as a route into explaining and discussing matters of content.
◆ Candidates may be required to comment on other literary interpretations or readings.

Below are some possible ways of considering the language of poetry, which you can use as questions to ask of a poem, or triggers for discussion.

The nature of poetry

◆ the range of structures and techniques
◆ the discipline of the form
◆ any deviation from normal rules
◆ experimentation with words.

The function of poetry

Poetry can be any or all of the following:

◆ expressive
◆ entertaining
◆ emotional
◆ thought-provoking
◆ descriptive
◆ evaluative
◆ informative.

Features of poetry

◆ Manner – formal, informal
◆ Form and structure – ballad, sonnet, ode, blank verse, free verse etc.
◆ Poetic devices – enjambment, metre, rhythm, pauses, etc.
◆ Lexical choice (choice of words) – abstract or concrete nouns, verbs, dialect words etc.
◆ Grammar – sentence structure, tense, mood, etc.
◆ Metaphorical devices – imagery, metaphors, similes, symbolism
◆ Rhetorical techniques – phonological patterning, alliteration, onomatopoeia, repetition, rhyme, antithesis, listing, etc.
◆ Typography and layout – typographical and structural features, layout, etc.

Poetic intention

In addition to studying the features of poems it is important to consider what the poets want their poetry to do – the poetic intention.

Here are some types of poetic intention:

◆ to characterize – physical description, implied description, etc.
◆ to set the scene – use of tense, word order, sentence structure, metaphorical language, etc.
◆ to evoke atmosphere – use of lexis, tense connotation, sentence structure, etc.
◆ to experiment with language and structure – use of dialect, invented vocabulary, sounds, repetition, etc.

These are some aspects of poetry that may fruitfully be studied in preparation for an exam, but it is *essential* that the features of language are studied with reference to the poems themselves. The only purpose of identifying features a poet might use is to look at the effects they create within the poem and how these contribute to its expression. You can then evaluate the success of these features in terms of the effects they have on the impact of the poem overall and therefore on the reader.

We can begin by looking at two extracts from Chaucer's *The Miller's Tale*. Potential questions for an examination could focus on a range of features in Chaucer's language and how he uses these to achieve his desired effects.

For example, one favourite area that examiners often write questions about in relation to Chaucer's poetry is its variety – the different techniques he uses in terms of poetic devices, creation of character, creation of scene and atmosphere, comic scenes, poetic voice, and so on. A question on this area could take this form:

> '*The Miller's Tale* demonstrates the richness and enormous variety of Chaucer's English'. How far do you agree with this statement? You should make detailed reference to the range of stylistic features that Chaucer uses and the effects that these create within the poetry.

As *The Miller's Tale* is a richly comic tale, another favourite area of questioning focuses on how the comedy is created and what kind of comedy it is. This type of question might start by drawing your attention to a particular part of the text in which something comic happens. You are then asked to examine the ways in which the language is used in that section to create a comic effect. Sometimes the question might contain a second element that broadens it to take account of the whole text, for example: 'How far do you agree with the view that *The Miller's Tale* is little more than a collection of comic scenes and circumstances?'

A third aspect of this tale which often crops up in examination questions is Chaucer's characterization. The debate usually centres on a) the techniques that Chaucer uses to create his characters and b) the extent to which they are fully rounded characters, or are caricatures. The two extracts below focus on this area. The first one describes Alisoun and the second, Absolom.

Text 1

THE MILLER'S TALE

This carpenter hadde wedded newe a wyf,
Which that he lovede moore than his lyf;
Of eighteteene yeer she was of age.

Jalous he was, and heeld hire narwe in cage,
For she was wylde and yong, and he was old
And demed hymself been lik a cokewold.
He knew nat Catoun, for his wit was rude,
That bad man sholde wedde his simylitude.
Men sholde wedden after hire estaat,
For youthe and elde is often at debaat.
But sith that he was fallen in the snare,
He moste endure, as oother folk, his care.
Fair was this yonge wyf, and therwithal
As any wezele hir body gent and smal.
A ceynt she werede, barred al of silk,
A barmclooth as whit as morne milk
Upon hir lendes, ful of many a goore.
Whit was hir smok, and broyden al bifoore
And eek bihynde, on hir coler aboute,
Of col-blak silk, withinne and eek withoute.
The tapes of hir white voluper
Were of the same suyte of hir coler;
Hir filet brood of silk, and set tul hye.
And sikerly she hadde a likerous ye;
Ful smale ypulled were hire browes two,
And tho were bent and blake as any sloo.
She was ful moore blisful on to see
Than is the newe pere-jonette tree,
And softer than the wolle is of a wether.
And by hir girdel heeng a purs of lether,
Tasseled with silk and perled with latoun.
In al this world, to seken up and doun,
There nys no man so wys that koude thenche
So gay a popelote or swich a wenche.
Ful brighter was the shynyng of hir hewe
Than in the Tour the noble yforged newe.
But of hir song, it was as loude and yerne
As any swalwe sittynge on a beme.
Therto she koude skippe and make game,
As any kyde or calf folwynge his dame.
Hir mouth was sweete as bragot or the meeth,
Or hoord of apples leyd in hey or heeth.
Wynsynge she was, as is a joly colt,
Long as a mast, and upright as a bolt.
A brooch she baar upon hir lowe coler,
As brood as is the boos of a bokeler.
Hir shoes were laced on hir legges hye.
She was a prymerole, a piggesnye,
For any lord to leggen in his bedde,
Or yet for any good yeman to wedde.

Text 2

THE MILLER'S TALE

Now was ther of that chirche a parissh clerk,
The which that was ycleped Absolon.
Crul was his heer, and as the gold it shoon,
And strouted as a fanne large and brode;
Ful streight and evene lay his joly shode.
His rode was reed, his eyen greye as goos.
With Poules wyndow corven on his shoos,
In hoses rede he wente fetisly.
Yclad he was ful smal and proprely
Al in a kirtel of a lyght waget;
Ful faire and thikke been the poyntes set.
And therupon he hadde a gay surplys
As whit as is the blosme upon the rys.
A myrie child he was, so God me save.
Wel koude he laten blood, and clippe and shave,
And maken a chartre or lond or acquitaunce.
In twenty manere koude he trippe and daunce
After the scole of Oxenforde tho,
And with his legges casten to and fro,
And pleyen songes on a smal rubible;
Therto he song som tyme a loud quynyble;
And as wel koude he pleye on a giterne.
In al the toun nas brewhous ne taveme
That he ne visited with his solas,
Ther any gaylard tappestere was.
But sooth to seyn, he was somdeel squaymous
Of fartyng, and of speche daungerous.

Analytical tasks

1   Look at Text 1. Make a list of words and phrases that you find particularly effective in describing Alisoun. Describe the effect that each of these words or phrases has and the picture that they create.

2   Chaucer uses a number of images to describe Alisoun. Many of these are on the same theme. What are they, and how effective do you find them in terms of the overall description?

3   What is the effect of the closing lines of the description?

4   Look at Text 2. Make a list of the words or phrases that you find particularly effective in describing Absolom. Describe the effect that each of these words or phrases has and the picture that they create.

Points of linguistic interest

Text 1

◆ the use of animal imagery
◆ the detailed description of her clothing
◆ reference to *'lendes'*, *'Likerous ye'*
◆ descriptive terms such as *'prymerole'*, *'piggesnye'* and *'popelote'* and their implications.

Text 2

◆ the description of Absolon's hair and its implications
◆ the effects of words such as *'rode'*, *'Quynyble'* and *'daungerous'*
◆ the description of his clothing.

Assignment

Examine the ways in which Chaucer uses language in each of these descriptions in order to create a sense of character. You should focus particularly on Chaucer's use of vocabulary and imagery, and the connotations of some of the terms that he uses.

Text 3

Now we will look at a rather different kind of poem, *A Meterorite*, from *The Dead Sea Poems* by Simon Armitage. Although six hundred years separates the writing of *The Miller's Tale* and *A Meteorite*, your job in terms of answering exam questions on them is the same. You need to look at the ways in which the poet has used language in certain ways in order to create the effects he desires. On a text like *The Dead Sea Poems*, the examiner is likely to set one question that addresses broad issues, such as the following:

> Explore the ways in which Armitage uses the experiences of domestic life in his poetry. Your answer should embrace linguistic as well as thematic concerns and should include a discussion of his use of form, style and vocabulary.

The second question may well focus on an individual poem and ask you to look at the way language is used here, and then to broaden your comments to some of the other poems in the anthology.

A METEORITE

So what, a piece of flint, a cinder, set
within the ring or pincers of my thumb
and index finger, like a precious stone.

Just so, precisely that, although
there's nothing other-worldly here, no hot
unstable element or compound, not
one point or dot or grain to place this rock
in outer space, no property or part
belonging to some other moon or star
known by a number rather than a name.

Not even a trace of Robinsonite,
unearthed in the Red Bird mercury mine
and christened by him whose crystalline find
was dust in his hand on coming to light.

But something all the same, for having flown
so far, found land, for having come to hand,
and put that way there's hardly anything
this piece can't say. A line of plot, a script,
and there and then this rock becomes a gem,
a gift; your fingers open, slowly, like
a flower, from a fist. As if. As if.

Analytical tasks

1 Work through the poem, stanza by stanza, and make brief notes on what the poem appears to be about.

2 Make a list of the images that Armitage uses and describe the effects that they create.

3 Make notes on the way in which Armitage structures the poem.

4 Do you think he has used either rhythm or rhyme to any particular effect in this poem?

Points of linguistic interest

◆ the dismissive opening
◆ the structure of the poem
◆ the range of vocabulary and use of imagery
◆ the ending of the poem.

Assignment

With reference to *A Meteorite*, discuss the ways in which Simon Armitage uses language here and elsewhere in the collection. Your answer should include a discussion of the ways in which language choices affect meaning.

(If you have not studied this text, obviously your discussion will focus on only *A Meteorite*.)

You will have noted from the introduction to this section that one of the things that you might be required to do is to 'comment on other interpretations and readings'. The next set of extracts will enable you to practise this skill. *La Belle Dame Sans Merci* by John Keats is followed by two extracts from critical works on Keats.

Text 4

LA BELLE DAME SANS MERCI

I
O what can ail thee, knight-at-arms,
Alone and palely loitering?
The sedge has wither'd from the lake,
And no birds sing.

II
O what can ail thee, knight-at-arms,
So haggard and so woe-begone?
The squirrel's granary is full,
And the harvest's done.

III
I see a lilly on thy brow,
With anguish moist and fever dew,
And on thy cheeks a fading rose
Fast withereth too.

IV
I met a lady in the meads,
Full beautiful — a faery's child,
Her hair was long, her foot was light,
And her eyes were wild.

V
I made a garland for her head,
And bracelets too, and fragrant zone;
She look'd at me as she did love,
And made sweet moan.

VI
I set her on my pacing steed
And nothing else saw all day long,
For sidelong would she bend, and sing
A faery's song.

VII
She found me roots of relish sweet,
And honey wild, and manna dew,
And sure in language strange she said —
'I love thee true'.

VIII
She took me to her elfin grot,
And there she wept, and sigh'd full sore,
And there I shut her wild wild eyes
With kisses four.

IX
And there she lulled me asleep,
And there I dream'd – Ah! woe betide! –
The latest dream I ever dream'd
On the cold hill side.

X
I saw pale kings and princes too,
Pale warriors, death-pale were they all;
They cried – 'La Belle Dame sans Merci
Hath thee in thrall!'

XI
I saw their starved lips in the gloam,
With horrid warning gaped wide,
And I awoke and found me here,
On the cold hill's side.

XII
And this is why I sojourn here,
Alone and palely loitering,
Though the sedge has wither'd from the lake,
And no birds sing.

John Keats (1795–1821)

Text 5

This text is from Brian Stone's *The Poetry of Keats*.

And so to 'La Belle Dame Sans Merci', the title of which Keats took from an early fifteenth-century French poem by Alain Charlier. The phrase belongs to the terminology of courtly love, and describes a beautiful lady without 'mercy', that is, the sort of gracious kindness which prompts a woman to accept a lover's pleas.

With its haunting medieval resonances, the poem is the last of those for which Keats drew on the literature and folklore of the Middle Ages. Much may be said of the sources of its ideas and images, but it is difficult, and perhaps unwise to attempt, to be specific about its final meaning. In this respect it may be approached and experienced in much the same way as Blake's poem 'The Sick Rose', which also raises, by powerful images and in even much briefer compass, ideas of love, corruption and death.

The narrative thrust of the poem places it at once as an evocation of the medieval supernatural ballad, one characteristic of which is the seduction by one of the faery folk of a human being, who loses his or her freedom or life in consequence. Such are Clerk Colvill, Tarn Lin and especially Thomas the Rhymer, the last of whom was an actual poet of Erceldoune in Scotland who lived in the thirteenth century. The versification and the process of narration by dialogue show Keats to be deeply imbued with the spirit and techniques of the medieval ballad. Keats's first poetic master, Spenser, also wrote about enchantresses from the medieval worlds of ballad and Arthurian literature, one of whom, Duessa, figures strongly in Book I of *The Faerie Queene*. She may be a foretype of Keats's 'belle dame', who takes the power out of men by luring them into making love.

The further medieval reference in the poem concerns the idea of a waste land which might be made productive again by the action of a virtuous knight, as in the Grail legends. At the start of the poem the questioner of the haggard and woebegone knight-at-arms speaks in a winter landscape, from which the birds have departed:

> The sedge has wither'd from the lake.
> And no birds sing!
>
> The squirrel's granary is full,
> And the harvest's done.

But, as she seduces the knight, La Belle Dame feeds him with such choice natural products as 'honey wild, and manna dew' . That plenty is part of the enchantment which lures him to the act of love, and to the ensuing sleep in her arms in which, with the sudden chill of nightmare, he

> . . . saw pale kings, and princes too,
> Pale warriors, death-pale were they all;
> They cried – 'La Belle Dame sans Merci
> Hath thee in thrall!'

The 'horrid warning' uttered by the 'starved lips' of the nightmare figures – and 'starved' here means, as in Shakespeare, 'starved to death' – confirms that the lady is a murderous enchantress. As the knight is seen by the questioner in a state of decay, perhaps because he was active and willing in his own seduction, it is suggested that he is responsible for the corruption of his essence, perhaps to the point of bringing on his death:

I see a lily on thy brow,
With anguish moist and fever-dew,
And on thy cheek a fading rose
Fast withereth too.

The five-fold repetition of 'pale' links the poem firmly with 'As Hermes once' in considering the act of love in connection with death. It is as if the knight was taken beyond life, saw in the hereafter others who, like himself, had been seduced by the enchantress, and was returned to this world weakened and corrupted past cure by his experience.

It seems that, whether or not the poem is an expression of Keats's guilt about love, it does present a complex image of his state of mind. Robert Graves expresses one view: 'That the Belle Dame represented Love, Death by Consumption . . . and Poetry all at once can be confirmed by a study of the romances from which Keats derived the poem' (*The White Goddess*, 1948). This idea of the enchantress being a sort of 'demon muse' is supported by Katherine M. Wilson in *The Nightingale and the Hawk: A Psychological Study of Keats's Odes* (1964) and there is some evidence from Keats's letters and our knowledge of his life to support Graves's opinion. Twice in his last two years, when desperately in love with Fanny Brawne, he put himself at a distance from her in order to make sure that he could concentrate on composing poetry: and that indicates strife between his two major impulses, which were to fulfil both his destiny as a poet and his love for her. Then, the connection between love and thoughts about death, is a permanent feature of Keats's cast of mind, and of his poetry.

Some of the images in the poem, including those of the rose and the lily, come from the section on Love-Melancholy in Burton's *Anatomy of Melancholy*, Keats's copy of which is marked accordingly. But all these ideas should be held in solution. It is the wholeness of the poem, with its hypnotically enforced suggestion and concentrated associations, which impresses itself on the reading and rereading of 'La Belle Dame Sans Merci'. It permanently haunts the mind with the music of its particular tragic themes, which need not be referred outside the poem itself.

Text 6

The next extract is by Peter Cairns, and is from 'The sense of transience in the poems of 1819', in *Keats: Poems and Letters*, ed. Cookson and Loughrey.

. . . in 'La Belle Dame sans Merci', the sad or menacing rhythms are largely the effect of a shorter last line. The simple language and the apparent simplicity of the ballad form help to establish the medieval setting and to suggest the ingenuous recounting of a dream-like experience, as in Coleridge's ballad *The Rime of the Ancient Mariner*. However, the feel of this poem is very different. This is not only because of the stillness of the scene: it is due to the rhythmic effect of the last line, often only four syllables long, but usually containing three heavy stresses. The effect is to slow the rhythm to a pause each time, but also of words echoing in a silence. Also the stressed words are those which convey most emotively the menacing approach of winter or death, particularly at the beginning and end of the poem:

> And no birds sing. (stanza I)
> And the harvest's done. (stanza II)
> Fast withereth too. (stanza III)

Two lines are used twice, with haunting effect in the last two stanzas:

> On the cold hill's side. (stanza XI)
> And no birds sing. (stanza XII)

In his lyrical ballad then, Keats employs most effectively the two structural devices of framing and cadence to convey the doomed quality of human happiness. Robert Gittings, who in his book *The Living Year* (London, 1954) writes interestingly about the background to these poems suggests:

> The story 'La Belle Dame' is, among all its other elements, the story of Keats's dead brother and the cruel deception that first his friends, and then life itself, had played upon him – the delivery of his youth to disappointment and death. It gains for us its poignancy . . . from a circumstance unseen to Keats – that within two years he himself was to go the way of his brother and to join him among the death-pale crowd.

Analytical tasks

1 Make notes on the poem covering the following aspects:

- ◆ what the poem means to you
- ◆ any images or descriptions that strike you as particularly effective, and the effect they have on the poem
- ◆ the structure, rhythm and rhyme patterns of the poem.

2 Look at Text 5. What are the main points that Stone makes about the poem?

3 Look at Text 6. What are the main points that Cairns makes about the poem?

4 Think again about your own response to the poem. What comments would you make about the two readings that you have looked at? Have they made you reconsider your own interpretation at all?

Points of linguistic interest

- ◆ the use of the medieval ballad form
- ◆ the use of a variety of images
- ◆ the connotations of death in the vocabulary used
- ◆ the use of repetition.

Student response

In 'La Belle Dame Sans Merci' the poet, Keats, appears to express his disillusionment with love through the central character, the knight. The poem opens with the knight appearing 'alone and palely loitering' and, as the poem goes on to tell us, this is as a result of his encounter with the enchantress. The knight appears to have been so besotted with the beauty of the 'lady' that he had succumbed to her enchantment, believing her, foolishly, when she tells him: 'I love thee true'. Near the end of the poem we find, through the knight's dream, that he is not the first man of noble standing to be deceived by the temptress: 'I saw pale kings and princes too, / Pale warriors death-pale were they all.' Ignoring their 'horrid warning' we see the eventual demise of the knight, who appears to have been deceived by 'love', thus suggesting the poet's own disillusionment.

The medieval period in history conjures up romantic images of noble, valiant knights who fought for moral good. By using a medieval setting, therefore, the apparent 'fall' of the knight is heightened. Keats succeeds in creating this medieval flavour, which also adds a mystical tone to the poem, through his use of language and form. The medieval ballad is generally constructed in story form through short, simple stanzas, sometimes being a lyrical account of actual events, perhaps containing a moralistic element. Keats uses this ballad form to relate the somewhat moralistic tale of the knight and the enchantress.

There is a strong sense of transience about the poem which supports the notion of the poet's own disillusionment with love. For example, images such as the 'fading rose', supported by the phrase, 'fast withereth', enhance the idea that beauty, like love, is destined to be short-lived. The cyclical nature of the poem is also suggestive of this transience. After the opening two stanzas which see the knight in a somewhat barren environment: 'the sedge has wither'd from the lake, / And no birds sing', the poem goes on to display a wealth of lush imagery: 'she found me roots of relish sweet, / And honey wild, and manna dew', before returning to the same barren imagery in the final stanza.

To create a mystical, supernatural feel to the poem, Keats includes phrases such as: 'a faery's child' and 'elfin grot'. In addition, Keats adds a dark, foreboding tone through his use of language, suggesting that the knight's apparent pleasure in being seduced will be short-lived. For example, the poet describes the maiden's beauty but adds: 'her eyes were wild', and even her words: 'I love thee true' were spoken in a 'language strange'. The rhythm too gives an indication of discord as the fast-flowing pace of the first three lines of each stanza is slowed by the final line which succeeds in breaking the flow of the poem overall.

→

If we see love itself being personified in the enchantress – who has the ability to enthral, 'and nothing else saw all day long', who can dis-empower, 'And there she lulled me asleep', and who is seen to be able to destroy through her departure, 'And I awoke and found me here, / On the cold hill's side . . . Alone and palely loitering' – we can recognize the disillusionment with love that the poet expresses. Love, like the Belle Dame, has no mercy.

Question 2

In this extract, Brian Stone makes a number of points:

- He focuses on the title of the poem claiming, 'the phrase belongs to the terminology of courtly love'.
- Stone identifies medieval folklore as a major influence on the poem.
- He highlights the ambiguity of the poem's meaning, stating that it is '. . . unwise to attempt to be specific about its final meaning'.
- He uses comparisons with other poems – 'The Sick Rose' by William Blake, for example.
- Stone alludes to the fact the Keats' 'belle dame' finds her origin to be in Spenser's Duessa, who 'takes power out of men by luring them into making love'.
- He mentions the contrast between the 'haggard and woebegone' knight at the beginning of the poem and the apparent richness and abundance surrounding the seduction. Stone sees 'That plenty' as 'part of the enchantment which lures him to the act of love'.
- He draws attention to the language of the poem – for example, the word 'starved'. He sees this word as being an indication that 'the lady is a murderous enchantress'.
- He also highlights the 'five-fold repetition of "pale"' stating that, in his view, this links love with death.
- Stone sees the knight as being a willing victim and therefore 'responsible for the corruption of his essence, perhaps to the point of bringing on his death'.
- He draws on other viewpoints about both the poem and the poet's own state of mind. Here he mentions Robert Graves, Katherine M. Wilson and Keats's own letters.
- Stone also looks at Keats's relationship with Fanny Brawne and his comment that 'he put himself at a distance from her in order to make sure that he could concentrate on composing poetry' leads Stone to propose that his love for her and his work as a poet were two major, but conflicting, aspects of his life.

Question 3

In the second extract, Cairns makes the following points:

- He focuses on the rhythm patterns evident within the poem,

→

> highlighting the way that the final line of each stanza achieves a slowing of pace. This, he suggests, creates the effect of 'slow(ing) the rhythm to a pause'.
> ◆ He looks more closely at the rhythm pattern of the last line of each stanza, identifying their 'three heavy stresses', of which he states: 'the stressed words are those which convey most emotively the menacing approach of winter or death'.
> ◆ He looks at the repetition of lines and expresses his view that they enhance the poem's 'haunting' effect.
> ◆ Cairns points out that the poem is effective in conveying the 'doomed quality of human happiness'.
> ◆ He includes a quote by Robert Gittings whose interpretation of 'La Belle Dame Sans Merci' is that the poem, among other things, tells the story of 'Keats's dead brother'.
>
> <u>Question 4</u>
>
> It is interesting to see how Stone looks at the possible influences on the writing of 'La Belle Dame Sans Merci', especially through his references to other poems. Stone, like Cairns, sees in the poem the association between love and death, although Cairns tends to focus more on the poetic techniques apparent in the poem. On examining both extracts alongside my own response, it becomes clear that different interpretations of the poem appear equally valid. As Stone states: 'Much may be said of the sources of its ideas and images, but it is difficult, and perhaps unwise to attempt, to be specific about its final meaning.' ◆

Examiner's comments

The student shows a clear focus on this question right from the start and there is a sound awareness of the way in which language is working in the poem. She shows understanding of the narrative thread of the poem and the idea of deception, disappointment and disillusionment that lies behind it. The comments on the medieval context of the poem are interesting and give clear evidence that the student is aware of a broader contextual setting. It is particularly encouraging to see an appreciation of what lies behind the lines – the comments on the transient tone of the poem are particularly well-judged. We see a close focus on language, together with the effects of imagery and personification.

The points made on Stone's comments about the poem reflect a sound understanding of what is being said, as well as an appreciation of the views of another reader.

Assignment

With detailed reference to *La Belle Dame Sans Merci*, examine the ways in which Keats uses language and form in order to capture the flavour of the medieval ballad, while at the same time exploring his own thematic interests. (If you wish, you can include your views about other interpretations where they have helped to inform your own.)

Text 7

Now we will have a look at some quite different poems. Grace Nichols was born in 1950 in Guyana, where she grew up. She came to Britain in 1977. She has published a number of books and one of the best known is her collection of poems, *The Fat Black Woman's Poems*. Most of the poems in this collection are fairly short and are written in straightforward language, although she does sometimes write in West Indian dialect form and sometimes uses West Indian terms. There are certain features of her work that exam questions tend to focus on. Her writing is full of life and in the persona of the 'Fat Black Woman' she creates a strong sense of character. Her use of imagery is also often striking, and it has been said of her that she '. . . gives us images that stare us straight in the eye, images of joy, challenge, accusation' and her use of language has been described as 'vivid and economical'. Through some of her poems she poses awkward questions to politicians and rulers and 'to a white world that still turns its back'. These are all rich areas that the examiner can draw upon for questions – for example:

> Beginning with a detailed consideration of *Tropical Death*, discuss how the writer creates the voice of the central character in this poem and examine how her poetic choices of form, style and vocabulary achieve this same outcome elsewhere in the collection.

Here is another poem by Grace Nichols.

BE A BUTTERFLY

Be a Butterfly
Don't be a kyatta-pilla
Be a butterfly
old preacher screamed
to illustrate his sermon
of Jesus and the higher life

rivulets of well-earned
sweat sliding down
his muscly mahogany face
in the half-empty school church
we sat shaking with muffling
laughter

watching our mother trying to save
herself from joining the wave

only our father remaining poker face
and afterwards we always went home to
split peas Sunday soup
with dumplings, fufu and pigtail

Don't be a kyatta-pilla
Be a butterfly
Be a butterfly

That was de life preacher
And you was right

Analytical tasks

1 Make notes on how the poem develops stanza by stanza.

2 Make a note of any particular images or descriptions that strike you as effective.

3 How do you think the structure contributes to the overall effect of the poem?

4 What other poetic devices or techniques does Nichols use in this poem, and how do they contribute to its effectiveness?

Points of linguistic interest

◆ kyatta-pilla – why not caterpillar?
◆ the imagery
◆ the structure (and rhyme)
◆ the use of upper and lower case.

Assignment

'Grace Nichols gives us images that stare us straight in the eye, images of joy, challenge, accusation'. How true have you found this to be in *Be a Butterfly* and elsewhere in the collection? You should consider Nichols's use of vocabulary and the metaphorical and phonological features of her poems.

Text 8

Christina Rossetti (1830–94) was a Victorian poet who wrote a wide range of different kinds of poetry. In a selection chosen for examination purposes you will find ballads, imaginative lively poems involving goblins and fairies, sonnets, and reflections on love and religion, death and heaven. Exam questions on Rossetti focus on various areas but she is noted for her love of verbal invention and metrical experimentation. In both her religious and secular poems there is a keen interest in natural, pictorial imagery, and her addresses to an unnamed lover or suitor often contain much ambiguity.

Here is a possible question focusing on the range of her poetry:

> Choose two poems that you have found very different in style, theme and structure from those studied. Examine the ways that Rossetti's use of language and structure creates the effects that she desired in each, and how you have found this typical of her work as a whole.

THE HEART KNOWETH ITS OWN BITTERNESS

When all the over-work of life
Is finished once, and fast asleep
We swerve no more beneath the knife
But taste that silence cool and deep;
Forgetful of the highways rough,
Forgetful of the thorny scourge,
Forgetful of the tossing surge,
Then shall we find it is enough?

How can we say 'enough' on earth —
'Enough' with such a craving heart?
I have not found it since my birth.
But still have bartered part for part.
I have not held and hugged the whole,
But paid the old to gain the new:
Much have I paid, yet much is due,
Till I am beggared sense and soul.

I used to labour, used to strive
For pleasure with a restless will:
Now if I save my soul alive
All else what matters, good or ill?
I used to dream alone, to plan
Unspoken hopes and days to come: —
Of all my past this is the sum —
I will not lean on child of man.

To give, to give, not to receive!
I long to pour myself, my soul,
Not to keep back or count or leave,
But king with king to give the whole.
I long for one to stir my deep —
I have had enough of help and gift —
I long for one to search and sift
Myself, to take myself and keep.

You scratch my surface with your pin,
You stroke me smooth with hushing breath: –
Nay pierce, nay probe, nay dig within,
Probe my quick core and sound my depth.
You call me with a puny call,
You talk, you smile, you nothing do:
How should I spend my heart on you,
My heart that so outweighs you all?

Your vessels are by much too strait;
Were I to pour, you could not hold. –
Bear with me! I must bear to wait,
A fountain seated through heat and cold.
Bear with me days or months or years:
Deep must call deep until the end
When friend shall no more envy friend
Nor vex his friend at unawares.

Not in this world of hope deferred.
This world of perishable stuff: –
Eye hath not seen nor ear hath heard
Nor heart conceived that full 'enough':
Here moans the separating sea,
Here harvests fail, here breaks the heart:
There God shall join and no man part,
I full of Christ and Christ of me.

Analytical tasks

1   Make notes stanza by stanza of what Rossetti is saying in this poem.

2   Examine the imagery that she uses. Make a note of images that strike you as particularly effective, and explain the effect that each creates in the poem.

3   What does the rhyme scheme and rhythm pattern contribute to the overall effect of the poem?

4   What is your assessment of the success of this poem in achieving the effects Rossetti desired?

Points of linguistic interest

◆ the reflective tone of the poem
◆ the imagery highlighting the harshness of life
◆ the relationship between the structure of the poem and the development of the ideas
◆ the effect of the rhyme scheme and the rhythm pattern.

Assignment

Examine the ways that Rossetti creates the tone and mood of this poem and contrast this against another poem from the collection where she creates a very different atmosphere. You should refer to her choice of vocabulary and her use of various stylistic techniques in your answer.

Examination assignment

Although the majority of Edward Thomas's poetry was written during the First World War – in fact he was killed in France by the blast of a shell at the start of the Battle of Arras in 1917 – the vast majority of his poetry is not concerned with war. At the heart of much of his poetry is the English countryside, which for him is intimately and inextricably tied up with memories and melancholy and a sense of the past.

Compare and contrast the two poems below, showing how Thomas uses language in each of them to achieve his effects. You should refer in detail to features such as vocabulary, metaphorical and rhetorical techniques, and structure in your answer.

Text A

THE MANOR FARM

The rock-like mud unfroze a little and rills
Ran and sparkled down each side of the road
Under the catkins wagging in the hedge.
But earth would have her sleep out, spite of the sun:
Nor did I value that thin gilding beam
More than a pretty February thing
Till I came down to the old Manor Farm,
And church and yew-tree opposite, in age
Its equals and in size. The church and yew
And farmhouse slept in a Sunday silentness.
The air raised not a straw. The steep farm roof,
With tiles duskily glowing, entertained
The mid-day sun: and up and down the roof
White pigeons nestled. There was no sound but one.
Three cart-horses were looking over a gate
Drowsily through their forelocks, swishing their tail
Against a fly, a solitary fly.

The Winter's cheek flushed as if he had drained
Spring, Summer, and Autumn at a draught
And smiled quietly. But 'twas not Winter –

Rather a season of bliss unchangeable
Awakened from farm and church where it had lain
Safe under tile and thatch for ages since
This England, Old already, was called Merry.

Text B

LIGHTS OUT

I have come to the borders of sleep,
The unfathomable deep
Forest where all must lose
Their way, however straight,
Or winding, soon or late;
They cannot choose.

Many a road and track
That, since the dawn's first crack,
Up to the forest brink,
Deceived the travellers,
Suddenly now blurs,
And in they sink.

Here love ends,
Despair, ambition ends;
All pleasure and all trouble,
Although most sweet or bitter,
Here ends in sleep that is sweeter
Than tasks most noble.

There is not any book
Or face of dearest look
That I would not turn from now
To go into the unknown
I must enter, and leave, alone,
I know not how.

The tall forest towers;
Its cloudy foliage lowers
Ahead, shelf above shelf;
Its silence I hear and obey
That I may lose my way
And myself.

3 The Language of Prose

Introduction

The third unit you will study for the AS element of your course is entitled 'The Study of the Language of Prose and Speech'. Section A of this unit will involve Prose Study – you will study one prose text selected from those given in the specification.

This section provides you with a variety of exam-style questions on different texts. If you have not studied these texts, you can use the passages as practice in looking at the different ways writers use language – they are all self-contained pieces. If you have studied the text, however, you can answer further questions of the kind you are likely to face in the exam. Remember that in the exam this is a 'closed book' paper, but a passage from the text you have studied will be printed on the paper so that you can answer questions involving close analysis of a particular part of the text. It is likely that the question will ask you to discuss wider aspects of the text, too. You should look upon the extract, therefore, as a route into consideration of the whole text.

It will help you tackle exam questions if you take a methodical approach to your study of a prose text. This unit focuses on the ways in which language is used in prose texts, and so **purpose** and **audience** are key issues here. The following outline is one way of formulating responses to the variety of question types that could be asked.

Frameworks

◆ Briefly identify what determines use of language, e.g. audience, purpose, genre and mode
◆ Focus on literary and linguistic frameworks as necessary.

Analysis and explanation

◆ Identify, exemplify and explain the values and attitudes of the author
◆ Describe the features of the text, e.g. character, ideas, themes and issues
◆ Consider meaning(s) and effect.

Evaluation

◆ Briefly consider the writer's success.

The specification offers the following advice:

◆ Candidates will be asked to show how language is used and developed by the writer within a text
◆ Candidates will be asked to refer to a specific section of the text, then widen and contextualize their study and analysis from that section
◆ Candidates may be asked how literary issues are raised by the writer.

Here is a possible approach that you might find useful, and questions to ask in considering a piece of narrative prose.

Features of narrative prose

◆ **manner** – formal or informal?
◆ **viewpoint** – first person, third person?
◆ **narrator** – intrusive, unintrusive, reliable, unreliable?
◆ **lexis** – e.g. noun/verb choice, modifiers etc.
◆ **speech** – e.g. direct/indirect, etc.
◆ **grammar** – e.g. tense, mood, syntax
◆ **metaphorical language** – e.g. imagery, metaphor, similes, symbolism
◆ **rhetorical techniques** – e.g. juxtaposition, listing, parallelism, patterning, etc.

The function of narrative prose

◆ language use is **expressive**
◆ one of its main functions is to **entertain**
◆ other purposes are to **educate** and **inform**.

Authorial intention

◆ to characterize
◆ to set the scene
◆ to evoke atmosphere
◆ to experiment with language.

These are some of the aspects of prose that may fruitfully be studied in preparation for an exam, but it is *essential* that the features of language are studied with reference to the prose texts themselves. The only purpose of identifying features a writer might use is to look at the effects they create within the text and how these contribute to its overall effectiveness. You can then evaluate their success in terms of their impact on the text as a whole and therefore on the reader.

Text 1

We can begin by looking at an extract from *Beloved* by Toni Morrison. In the extract that follows we see Beloved at a point of primary identification with her mother. The nature of this kind of narrative does not always make meaning obvious or easy to grasp.

BELOVED

I am Beloved and she is mine. I see her take flowers away from leaves   she put them in a round basket   the leaves are not for her   she fills the basket   she opens the grass   I would help her but the clouds are in   die way   how can I say things that are pictures   I am not separate from her   there is no place where I stop   her face is my own and I want to be there in the place where her face is and to be looking at it too   a hot thing

All of it is now   it is always now   there will never be a time when I am not crouching and watching others who are crouching too   I am always crouching the man on my face is dead   his face is not mine   his mouth smells sweet but his eyes are locked   some who eat nasty themselves   I do not eat   the men without skin bring us their morning water to drink   we have none   at night I cannot see the dead man on my face   daylight comes through the cracks and I can see his locked eyes   I am not big   small rats do not wait for us to sleep someone is thrashing but there is no room to do it in   if we had more to drink we could make tears   we cannot make sweat or morning water so the men without skin bring us theirs   one time they bring us sweet rocks to suck   we are all trying to leave our bodies behind   the man on my face has done it   it is hard to make yourself die forever   you sleep short and then return   in me beginning we could vomit   now we do not   now we cannot   his teeth are pretty white points   someone is trembling   I can feel it over here   he is fighting hard to leave   his body which is a small bird trembling   there is no room to tremble so he is not able to die   my own dead man is pulled away from my face   I miss his pretty white points

We are not crouching now   we are standing but my legs are like my dead man's eyes   I cannot fall because there is no room to   the men without skin are making loud noises   I am not dead   the bread is sea-colored   I am too hungry to eat it   the sun closes my eyes   those able to die are in a pile   I cannot find my man   the one whose teeth I have loved   a hot thing   the little hill of dead people   a hot thing   the men without skin push them through with poles   me woman is there with roe face I want   the face that is mine they fall into the sea which is the color of the bread   she has nothing in her ears   if I had the teeth of the man who died on my face I would bite the circle around her neck   bite it away   I know she does not like it   now there is room to crouch and to watch the crouching others   it is the crouching that is now always now   inside   the woman with my face is in the sea   a hot thing

In the beginning I could see her   I could not help her because the clouds were in the way   in the beginning I could see her   the shining in her ears   she does not like the circle around her neck   I know this   I look hard at her so she will know that the clouds are in the way   I am sure she saw me   I am looking at her see me   she empties out her eyes   I am there in the place where her face is and telling her the noisy clouds were in my way she wants her ear-rings she wants her round basket   I want her face   a hot thing

In the beginning the women are away from the men and the men are away from the women   storms rock us and mix the men into the women and the women into the men   that is when I begin to be on the back of the man   for a long time I see only his neck and his wide shoulders above me   I am small   I love him because he has a song   when he turned around to die I see the teeth he sang through   his singing was soft   his singing is of the place where a woman takes flowers away from their leaves and puts them in a round basket before the clouds   she is crouching near us   but I do not see her until he locks his eyes and dies on my face   we are that way   there is no breath coming from his mouth and the place where breath should be is sweet-smelling   the others do not know he is dead   I know   his song is gone   now I love his pretty little teeth instead

I cannot lose her again   my dead man was in the way like the noisy clouds when he dies on my face I can see hers   she is going to smile at me   she is going to   her sharp earrings are gone   die men without skin are making loud noises   they push my own man through   they do not push the woman with my face through   she goes in   they do not push her   she goes in   the little hill is gone   she was going to smile at me   she was going to   a hot thing

They are not crouching now   we are   they are floating on the water   they break up the little hill and push it through   I cannot find my pretty teeth   I see the dark face that is going to smile at me   it is my dark face that is going to smile at me   the iron circle is around our neck   she does not have sharp earrings in her ears or a round basket   she goes in the water   with my face.

Analytical tasks

1 Write down the **impressions** that you get from reading this extract. Don't worry about whether they make any sense – concentrate on the images or connotations or associations raised by the words Morrison uses here.

2 Now review your impressions– does any idea or pattern begin to emerge?

3 Why do you think Morrison spaced out her writing in this way? Does it add anything to the overall impact when you read it?

4 What **effect** do you think Morrison wanted to achieve on her readers through writing in this way? Do you think this style is successful in achieving the effects she wanted?

Points of linguistic interest

◆ stream of consciousness or interior monologue technique
◆ even at a typographical level, disregards normal rules of writing
◆ viewpoint is infantile and incomplete

- sea-voyage as metaphor – perhaps the story of the slaves who came to America from Africa
- deliberately disorientates the reader.

Assignment

Here Morrison disregards the normal rules of written English in order to achieve her effects. Discuss her purpose, her achievements and how successful this techniques is both here and elsewhere in the novel. In your answer you should analyse and discuss:

- the ways in which the writer's attitudes and values are conveyed to the reader
- features of language such as vocabulary, punctuation and grammar
- the context of the extract and the whole novel.

Text 2

The following passage is from *The Railway Man* by Eric Lomax. Lomax was a prisoner in a Japanese prisoner of war camp during the Second World War. The extract describes a punishment beating inflicted on him for drawing a map of the railway.

THE RAILWAY MAN

Suddenly the NCO grabbed my shoulder and pulled me out, half stumbling, the relentless force in his powerful arm, his fingers pinching my flesh where he grabbed my shirt. I remember seeing the yard, and the river bank, and the wide brown river flowing past as we stood there. I remember seeing the cages, and noticing Major Smith and Mac and Slater, and seeing that Thew and Smith were now in cages too. But I was told fifty years later, by someone who should know, that I was first taken to a bathroom, and that there was a big metal tub in it, full of water, and that my head was shoved under the water again and again. I believe my informant, but to this day I can't honestly say I remember this. Nothing: a strange selective filter allows us to hold some things back from ourselves. But I do remember the rest.

A bench had been placed out in the open. I was told by the interpreter to lie down on it, and I lay on my front to protect my bandaged arms by wrapping them under the seat. But the NCO quickly hauled me upright again and made me lie on my back while he tied me to the bench with a rope. My arms were loose. The questioning recommenced. The interpreter's voice: 'Lomax, you will tell us why you made the map. You will tell us why you made a map of the railway. Lomax, were you in contact with the Chinese?'

The NCO picked up a big stick, a rough tree branch. Each question from the small man by my side was immediately followed by a terrible blow with the branch from above the height of the NCO's head on to my chest and stomach. It is so much worse when you see it coming like that, from above, when it is slow and deliberate. I used my splinted arms to try to protect my body, and the branch smashed on to them again and again. The interpreter was at my shoulder. 'Lomax, you will tell us. Then it will stop.' I think I felt his hand on my hand: a strange gesture, the obscene contrast between this gesture almost of comfort and the pitiless violence of what they were doing to me.

It is difficult to say how long the beating lasted, but for me it went slowly on for far too long. The NCO suddenly stopped hitting me. He went off to the side and I saw him coming back holding a hosepipe dribbling with water. From the facility with which he produced it and the convenient proximity of a water tap I guess he had used it before.

He directed the full flow of the now gushing pipe on to my nostrils and mouth at a distance of only a few inches. Water poured down my windpipe and throat and filled my lungs and stomach. The torrent was unimaginably choking. This is the sensation of drowning, on dry land, on a hot dry afternoon. Your humanity bursts from within you as you gag and choke. I tried very hard to will unconsciousness, but no relief came. He was too skilful to risk losing me altogether. When I was choking uncontrollably, the NCO took the hose away. The flat, urgent voice of the interpreter resumed above my head, speaking into my ear; the other man hit me with the branch on the shoulders and stomach a few more times. I had nothing to say; I was beyond invention. So they turned on the tap again, and again there was that nausea of rising water from inside my bodily cavity, a flood welling up from within and choking me.

They alternated beatings and half-drownings for I know not how long. No one was ever able to tell me how long all this lasted, and I have no idea whether it finished that day, or there was more the following day. I eventually found myself back in my cage. I must have been dragged there.

After dark – perhaps that same evening, or was it some other evening? How can I be a reliable witness about time? – the Kempei NCO made a special journey to my cage and handed through the bars a mug of hot milk, made with sweetened condensed milk. This was an incredible delight, but even at the time I knew it was not an act of kindness: it was a way of maintaining ambiguity, of keeping a prisoner off-balance.

Analytical tasks

1   What impact do you think that Lomax wanted this piece of writing to have on his readers?

2   How does Lomax create a sense of tension here?

3   Pick out any words or phrases that you find particularly effective and explain the effect they have had on you.

4   What is the effect of the final paragraph?

Points of linguistic interest

◆ the uncompromising description
◆ the use of similes and metaphors

◆ strong use of adjectives
◆ the structure of the extract – building to a climax and then down again.

Assignment

How does Lomax use language both in the extract and in the book as a whole, to give you a vivid impression of the suffering he underwent? In your answer you should comment on his use of:

◆ syntax
◆ vocabulary
◆ imagery
◆ structure.

Student response

Here is one student's response to this question. She had not read the whole book at the time she wrote this, and so her response is to the passage only.

The passage opens directly as Lomax emphasizes the roughness of his treatment – the way that the NCO grabs his shoulder, using terms like 'the relentless force', 'powerful arm', 'fingers pinching my flesh'. It emphasizes this treatment but it also creates a sense of tension too. He is being roughly treated here but how much worse is to come – this is only the beginning.

As Lomax writes in the first person we see things as if through his eyes as he is taken away, the yard and the river bank, the cages with the prisoners in them. He recollects the prisoners' names too, even though all this took place fifty years before. However, one thing that his memory does not recall is being taken to a bathroom and being semi-drowned in a tub a water. This touch again makes the whole experience seem real because in moments of real stress that is what the memory does sometimes – cuts out things that are too awful to bear.

It is clear that he has already been injured and his attempts to protect his already broken arms emphasizes his fragility and vulnerability. This sense is heightened still further as he is tied, face up, to the bench. The use of direct speech at this point is very effective as it makes real the voice of his interrogator. His voice sounds calm, almost polite, which, of course, makes it all the more menacing. Then comes the violence. The tension is increased as Lomax sees the NCO pick up a big stick. Then comes the juxtaposition of the soft, questioning voice, each question followed by a brutal blow. His attempts to use his splinted arms to try to protect himself adds pathos and intensifies the pain that he must have suffered, having blows fall on already broken arms.

→

> Again the pain is juxtaposed against the little gestures, almost of comfort from the interrogator – 'I think I felt his hand on my hand: a strange gesture, the obscene contrast between this gesture almost of comfort and the pitiless violence of what they were doing to me.' As if this is not enough they then start on the water torture. Lomax again describes this in detail and again the first-person narration makes it vivid and real to the reader. He does not know how long he endured these alternate beatings and drownings and again this brings a sense of realism – in those circumstances you can imagine reaching a point where you lose track of what is happening – as Lomax says himself 'How can I be a reliable witness about time?'
>
> At last, though, the beating ceases and the tension is released. Lomax is returned to his cage and then the NCO who had been torturing him brought him a mug of hot milk. Welcome though this is, Lomax knows that this is not an act of kindness but all part of their technique to keep the prisoner guessing.
>
> The overall structure of this extract starts by building up tension as we wait with Lomax for his ordeal to begin. Then it does, and his experience is described in detail in language which leaves the reader in no doubt as to the horror and brutality of his experience. He uses a range of sentence structures which keeps the pace going but also allows him to adjust it to suit the specific comment he is making. The use of direct speech not only varies the narrative but brings in the voice of the interrogator, which is not the brutal, harsh voice that we might imagine but a rather soft and polite one. The final paragraph brings down the tension again and gives the reader a break after the emotional intensity of what has just occurred. ◆

Examiner's comments

Although the student could have enlarged on a number of the points made and included more examples and illustrations, the response is sound overall. The student shows a good understanding both of Lomax's purpose and the effects he achieves and the techniques he uses to achieve them. Some of the analysis is quite subtle, and there is clear interplay between text and context. Here are specific strengths:

◆ the student identifies the use of first-person narrative and is aware of its effects
◆ she is aware of authorial intention
◆ she comments on his use of descriptive language (implicitly making a point about strong adjectives)
◆ she uses examples to support her points here
◆ she is also aware of Lomax's use of different syntactical patterns. Although she is not entirely secure about how to describe the effects, she is working towards an awareness of the impact of syntax on the piece.

Text 3

Now let us look at a quite different extract. This is taken from *Frankenstein* by Mary Shelley. In the extract below, the monster begins to narrate the history of his existence.

FRANKENSTEIN

'It is with considerable difficulty that I remember the original era of my being; all the events of that period appear confused and indistinct. A strange multiplicity of sensations seized me, and I saw, felt, heard, and smelt at the same time; and it was, indeed, a long time before I learned to distinguish between the operations of my various senses. By degrees, I remember, a stronger light pressed upon my nerves, so that I was obliged to shut my eyes. Darkness then came over me and troubled me, but hardly had I felt this when, by opening my eyes, as I now suppose, the light poured in upon me again. I walked and, I believe, descended, but I presently found a great alteration in my sensations. Before, dark and opaque bodies had surrounded me, impervious to my touch or sight; I now found that I could wander on at liberty, with no obstacles which I could not either surmount or avoid. The light became more and more oppressive to me, and the heat wearying me as I walked, I sought a place where I could receive shade. This was the forest near Ingolstadt; and here I lay by the side of a brook resting from my fatigue, until I felt tormented by hunger and thirst. This roused me from my nearly dormant state, and I ate some berries which I found hanging on the trees or lying on the ground. I slaked my thirst at the brook, and then lying down, was overcome by sleep.

'It was dark when I awoke; I felt cold also, and half frightened as it were, instinctively, finding myself so desolate. Before I quitted your apartment, on a sensation of cold, I had covered myself with some clothes, but these were insufficient to secure me from the dew of night. I was a poor, helpless, miserable wretch; I knew, and could distinguish, nothing; but feeling pain invade me on all sides, I sat down and wept.

'Soon a gentle light stole over the heavens and gave me a sensation of pleasure. I started up and beheld a radiant form rise from among the trees. I gazed with a kind of wonder. It moved slowly, but it enlightened my path, and I again went out in search of berries. I was still cold when under one of the trees I found a huge cloak, with which I covered myself, and sat down upon the ground. No distinct ideas occupied my mind: all was confused. I felt light, and hunger, and thirst, and darkness; innumerable sounds rang in my ears, and on all sides various scents saluted me: the only object that I could distinguish was the bright moon, and I fixed my eyes on that with pleasure.

'Several changes of day and night passed, and the orb of night had greatly lessened, when I began to distinguish my sensations from each other. I gradually saw plainly the clear stream that supplied me with drink and the trees that shaded me with their foliage. I was delighted when I first discovered that a pleasant sound, which often saluted my ears, proceeded from the throats of the little winged animals who had often intercepted the light from my eyes. I began also to observe, with greater accuracy, the forms that surrounded me, and to perceive the boundaries of the radiant roof of light which canopied me. Sometimes I tried to imitate the pleasant songs of the birds but was unable. Sometimes I wished to express my sensations in my own mode, but the uncouth and inarticulate sounds which broke from me frightened me into silence again.

'The moon had disappeared from the night, and again, with a lessened form, showed itself, while I still remained In the forest. My sensations had by this time become distinct, and my mind received every day additional ideas. My eyes became accustomed to the light and to perceive objects in their right forms: I distinguished the insect from the herb, and by degrees, one herb from another. I found that the sparrow uttered none but harsh notes, whilst those of the blackbird and thrush were sweet and enticing.

'One day, when I was oppressed by cold, I found a fire which had been left by some wandering beggars, and was overcome with delight at the warmth I experienced from it. In my joy I thrust my hand into the live embers, but quickly drew it out again with a cry of pain. How strange, I thought, that the same cause should produce such opposite effects! I examined the materials of the fire, and to my joy found it to be composed of wood. I quickly collected some branches, but they were wet and would not burn. I was pained at this and sat still watching the operation of the fire. The wet wood which I had placed near the heat dried and itself became inflamed. I reflected on this, and by touching the various branches, I discovered the cause and busied myself in collecting a great quantity of wood, that I might dry it and have a plentiful supply of fire. When night came on and brought sleep with it, I was in the greatest fear lest my fire should be extinguished. I covered it carefully with dry wood and leaves and placed wet branches upon it; and then, spreading my cloak, I lay on the ground and sank into sleep.

'It was morning when I awoke, and my first care was to visit the fire. I uncovered it, and a gentle breeze quickly fanned it into a flame. I observed this also and contrived a fan of branches, which roused the embers when they were nearly extinguished. When night came again I found, with pleasure, that the fire gave light as well as heat and that the discovery of this element was useful to me in my food, for I found some of the offals that the travellers had left had been roasted, and tasted much more savoury than the berries I gathered from the trees. I tried, therefore, to dress my food in the same manner, placing it on the live embers. I found that the berries were spoiled by this operation, and the nuts and roots much improved.'

Analytical tasks

1   What does the monster seem to be saying here?

2   How does Shelley create a sense of the monster's early memories being hazy?

3   What kind of image of the monster does she create here?

4   Pick out and comment on any words or phrases that strike you as effective.

Points of linguistic interest

◆ the use of first-person narration
◆ the lexical choices
◆ the creation of a sense of pathos
◆ the syntax and structure.

Assignment

Examine the extract and show how Shelley creates a sense of pathos for the monster both here and elsewhere in the novel. In your answer you should consider:

◆ the ways in which the writer's attitudes are conveyed to the reader
◆ the atmosphere created
◆ lexical and syntactical choice.

Text 4

The following extract is from *Hard Times* by Charles Dickens and describes Mrs Sparsit, Bounderby's housekeeper.

HARD TIMES

Mr Bounderby being a bachelor, an elderly lady presided over his establishment, in consideration of a certain annual stipend. Mrs Sparsit was this lady's name; and she was a prominent figure in attendance on Mr Bounderby's car, as it rolled along in triumph with the bully of humility inside.

For Mrs Sparsit had not only seen different days, but was highly connected. She had a great-aunt living in these very times called Lady Scadgers. Mr Sparsit, deceased, of whom she was the relict, had been by the mother's side what Mrs Sparsit still called 'a Powler.' Strangers of limited information and dull apprehension were sometimes observed not to know what a Powler was, and even to appear uncertain whether it might be a business, or a political party, or a profession of faith. The better class of minds, however, did not need to be informed that the Powlers were an ancient stock, who could trace themselves so exceedingly far back that it was not surprising if they sometimes lost themselves – which they had rather frequently done, as respected horseflesh, blind-hookey, Hebrew monetary transactions, and the Insolvent Debtors Court.

The late Mr Sparsit, being by the mother's side a Powler, married this lady, being by the father's side a Scadgers. Lady Scadgers (an immensely fat old woman, with an inordinate appetite for butcher's meat, and a mysterious leg which had now refused to get out of bed for fourteen years) contrived the marriage, at a period when Sparsit was just of age, and chiefly noticeable for a slender body, weakly supported on two long slim props, and surmounted by no head worth mentioning. He inherited a fair fortune from his uncle, but owed it all before he came into it, and spent it twice over immediately afterwards. Thus, when he died, at twenty-four (the scene of his decease, Calais, and the cause, brandy), he did not leave his widow, from whom he had been separated soon after the honeymoon, in affluent circumstances. That bereaved lady, fifteen years older than he, fell presently at deadly feud with her only relative, Lady Scadgers; and, partly to spite her ladyship, and partly to maintain herself, went out at a salary. And here she was, now, in her elderly days, with the Coriolanian style of nose and the dense black eyebrows which had captivated Sparsit, making Mr Bounderby's tea as he took his breakfast.

If Bounderby had been a conqueror, and Mrs Sparsit a captive princess whom he took about as a feature in his state-processions, he could not have made a greater flourish with her than he habitually did. Just as it belonged to his boastfulness to depreciate his own extraction, so it belonged to it to exalt Mrs Sparsit's. In the measure that he would not allow his own youth to have been attended by a single favourable circumstance, he brightened Mrs Sparsit's juvenile career with every possible advantage, and showered wagon-loads of early roses all over that lady's path. 'And yet, Sir,' he would say, 'how does it turn out after all? Why, here she is at a hundred a year (I give her a hundred, which she is pleased to term handsome), keeping the house of Josiah Bounderby of Coketown!'

Analytical tasks

1   What impression do you get of Mrs Sparsit?

2   How does Dickens use language to create a sense of her character?

3   Pick out any words or phrases that you find effective or interesting.

4   Write a brief character description of Mrs Sparsit.

Points of linguistic interest

◆ the use of adjectives
◆ the use of irony
◆ the use of imagery
◆ the use of humour.

Assignment

How does Dickens reveal his attitude towards Coketown and its inhabitants through his use of language in the novel? In your answer you should consider:

◆ the ways in which the writer's attitudes and values are conveyed to the reader
◆ some features of language such as vocabulary, imagery, and phonological aspects
◆ the context of the extract and the whole novel.

Text 5
....

The next extract is from *The Wasp Factory* by Iain Banks. Here we see the central character, Frank, stalking a buck rabbit with his airgun.

THE WASP FACTORY

I crawled quietly up the slope, the grass sliding under my chest and belly, my legs straining to propel my bulk up and forward. I was down-wind, of course, and the breeze was stiff enough to cover most small noises. As far as I could see, there were no rabbit sentries on the hill. I stopped about two metres down from the summit and quietly cocked the gun, inspecting the composite steel and nylon pellet before placing it in the chamber and snicking the gun closed. I closed my eyes and thought about the trapped, compressed spring and the little slug sitting at the shiny bottom of the rifled tube. Then I crawled to the top of the hill.

At first I thought I would have to wait. The Grounds looked empty in the afternoon light, and only the grass moved in the wind. I could see the holes and the little piles and scatters of droppings, and I could see the gorse bushes on the far slope above the bank which held most of the holes, where the rabbit-runs snaked tiny paths like jagged tunnels through the bushes, but there was no sign of the animals themselves. It was in those rabbit-runs through the gorse that some of the local boys used to set snares. I found the wire loops, though, having seen the boys set them, and I tore them out or put them under the grass on the paths the boys used to take when they came to inspect their traps. Whether any of them was tripped up by his own snare or not I don't know, but I'd like to think they did go sprawling head first. Anyway, they or their replacements don't set snares any more; I suppose it has gone out of fashion and they are out spraying slogans on walls, sniffing glue or trying to get laid.

Animals rarely surprise me but there was something about the buck, once I noticed it sitting there, that froze me for a second. It must have been there all the time, sitting motionless and staring straight at me from the far edge of the level area of the Grounds, but I hadn't noticed it at first. When I did, something about its stillness stilled me for a moment. Without actually moving physically, I shook my head clear inside and decided that the big male would make a fine head for a Pole. The rabbit might as well have been stuffed for all the movement it made, and I could see that it definitely was staring right at me, its little eyes not blinking, its tiny nose not sniffing, its ears untwitched. I stared straight back at it and very slowly brought the gun round to bear, moving it first one way then slightly the other, so that it looked like something swaying with the wind in the grass. It took about a minute to get the rifle in place and my head in the correct position, cheek by stock, and still the beast hadn't moved a millimetre.

Four times larger, his big whiskered head split neatly into four by the crosshairs, he looked even more impressive, and just as immobile. I frowned and brought my head up, suddenly thinking that it might just *be* stuffed; perhaps somebody was having a laugh at my expense. Town boys? My father? Surely not Eric yet? It was a stupid thing to have done; I'd moved my head far too quickly for it to look natural, and the buck shot off up the bank. I dipped my head and brought the gun up at the same time without thinking. There was no time to get back into the right position, take a breath and gently squeeze the trigger; it was up and bang, and with my whole body unbalanced and both hands on the gun I fell forward, rolling as I did so to keep the gun out the sand.

When I looked up, cradling the gun and gasping, my backside sunk in sand, I couldn't see the rabbit. I forced the gun down and hit myself on the knees. 'Shit!' I told myself.

The buck wasn't in a hole, however. It wasn't even near the bank where the holes were. It was tearing across the level ground in great leaps, heading right at me and seeming to shake and shiver in mid-air with every bound. It was coming at me like a bullet, head shaking, lips curled back, teeth long and yellow and by far the biggest I'd ever seen on a rabbit, live or dead. Its eyes looked like coiled slugs. Blobs of red arced from its left haunch with every pouncing leap; it was almost on me, and I was sat there staring.

There was no time to reload. By the time I started to react there was no time to do anything except at the instinctive level. My hands left the gun hanging in mid-air above my knees and went for the catapult, which as always was hanging on my belt, the arm-rest stuck down between that and my cords. Even my quick-reaction steelies were beyond reach in time, though; the rabbit was on me in a half-second, heading straight for my throat.

I caught it with the catapult, the thick black tubing of the rubber twisting once in the air as I scissored my hands and fell back, letting the buck go over my head and then kicking with my legs and turning myself so that I was level with it where it lay, kicking and struggling with the power of a wolverine, spreadeagled on the sand slope with its neck caught in the black rubber. Its head twisted this way and that as it tried to reach my fingers with its chopping teeth. I hissed through my own teeth at it and tugged the rubber tighter, then tighter still. The buck thrashed and spat and made a high keening noise I didn't think rabbits were capable of and beat its legs on the ground. I was so rattled I glanced round to make sure this wasn't a signal for an army of bunnies like this Dobermann of a beast to come up from behind and tear me to shreds.

The damn thing wouldn't die! The rubber was stretching and stretching and not tightening enough, and I couldn't move my hands for fear of it tearing the flesh off a finger or biting my nose off. The same consideration stopped me from butting the animal; I wasn't going to put my face near those teeth. I couldn't get

The novelist Iain Banks

a knee up to break its back, either, because I was almost slipping down the slope as it was, and I couldn't possibly get any purchase on that surface with only one leg. It was crazy! This wasn't Africa! It was a rabbit, not a lion! What the hell was happening here?

It finally bit me, twisting its neck more than I would have thought possible and catching my right index finger right on the knuckle.

That was it. I screamed and pulled with all my might, shaking my hands and my head and throwing myself backwards and over as I did so, banging one knee off the gun where it lay, fallen in the sand.

I ended up lying in the scrubby grass at the bottom of the hill, my knuckles white as I throttled the rabbit, swinging it in front of my face with its neck held on the thin black line of rubber tubing, now tied like a knot on a black string. I was still shaking, so I couldn't tell if the vibrations the body made were its or mine. Then the tubing gave way. The rabbit slammed into my left hand while the other end of the rubber whipped my right wrist; my arms flew out in opposite directions, crashing into the ground.

I lay on my back, my head on the sandy ground, staring out to the side where the body of the buck lay at the end of a little curved line of black, and tangled in the arm-rest and grip of the catapult. The animal was still.

I looked up at the sky and made a fist with the other hand, beating it into the ground, I looked back at the rabbit, then got up and knelt over it. It was dead; the head rolled slack, neck broken, when I lifted it. The left haunch was matted red with blood where my pellet had hit it. It was big; size of a tomcat; the biggest rabbit I'd ever seen.

Analytical tasks

1 Describe your first response when reading this extract.

2 Pick out any words, phrases or images that you have found particularly effective and comment on the writer's use of them.

3 Describe your impression of Frank and examine the ways in which Banks creates this impression through his use of language.

4 Discuss the way that Banks structures his account of this incident.

Points of linguistic interest

◆ the first-person narrative
◆ the use of imagery
◆ use of strong adjectives and adverbs
◆ the lexical and syntactical choices.

Assignment

How does the author construct a voice for Frank here, and elsewhere in the novel? In your answer you should consider:

◆ the ways in which the writer's attitudes and values are conveyed to the reader

> ◆ features of language such as vocabulary, imagery and syntax
> ◆ the narrative style.

Examination assignment

Read the passage printed below. The extract is taken from *Tess of the D'Ubervilles* by Thomas Hardy. Life at Flintcomb-Ash is hard, and Tess's life is an especially hard one.

Discuss the methods by which Hardy creates a sense of the environment and how this reflects the mood of Tess. In your answer you should consider:

◆ how the writer's attitudes and values are conveyed to the reader
◆ features of language such as use of vocabulary, syntax and structure
◆ the overall impact on the reader.

TESS OF THE D'URBERVILLES

There was no exaggeration in Marian's definition of Flintcomb-Ash farm as a starve-acre place. The single fat thing on the soil was Marian herself; and she was an importation. Of the three classes of village, the village cared for by its lord, the village cared for by itself, and the village uncared for either by itself or by its lord (in other words, the village of a resident squire's tenantry, the village of free or copy-holders, and the absentee-owner's village, farmed with the land) this place, Flintcomb-Ash, was the third.

But Tess set to work. Patience, that blending of moral courage with physical timidity, was now no longer a minor feature in Mrs Angel Clare; and it sustained her.

The swede-field in which she and her companion were set hacking was a stretch of a hundred odd acres, in one patch, on the highest ground of the farm, rising above stony lanchets or lynchets – the outcrop of siliceous veins in the chalk formation, composed of myriads of loose white flints in bulbous, cusped, and phallic shapes. The upper half of each turnip had been eaten off by the live-stock, and it was the business of the two women to grub up the lower or earthy half of the root with a hooked fork called a hacker, that it might be eaten also. Each leaf of the vegetable having already been consumed, the whole field was in colour a desolate drab; it was a complexion without features, as if a face, from chin to brow, should be only an expanse of skin. The sky wore, in another colour, the same likeness; a white vacuity of countenance with the lineaments gone. So these two upper and nether visages confronted each other all day long, the white face looking down on the brown face, and the brown face looking up at the white face, without anything standing between them but the two girls crawling over the surface of the former like flies. Nobody came near them, and their movements showed a mechanical regularity; their forms standing enshrouded in Hessian 'wroppers' – sleeved brown pinafores, tied behind to the bottom, to keep their gowns from blowing about – scant skirts revealing boots that reached high up the ankles, and yellow sheepskin gloves with gauntlets. The pensive character which the curtained hood lent to their bent heads would have reminded the observer of some early Italian conception of the two Marys.

They worked on hour after hour, unconscious of the forlorn aspect they bore in the landscape, not thinking of the justice or injustice of their lot. Even in such a position as theirs it was possible to exist in a dream. In the afternoon the rain came on again, and Marian said that they need not work any more. But if they did not work they would not be paid; so they worked on. It was so high a situation, this field, that the rain had no occasion to fall, but raced along horizontally upon the yelling wind, sticking into them like glass splinters till they were wet through. Tess had not known till now what was really meant by that. There are degrees of dampness, and a very little is called being wet through in common talk. But to stand working slowly in a field, and feel the creep of rain-water, first in legs and shoulders, then on hips and head, then at back, front, and sides, and yet to work on till the leaden light diminishes and marks that the sun is down, demands a distinct modicum of stoicism, even of valour.

Yet they did not feel the wetness so much as might be supposed. They were both young, and they were talking of the time when they lived and loved together at Talbothays Dairy, that happy green tract of land where summer had been liberal in her gifts: in substance to all, emotionally to these. Tess would fain not have conversed with Marian of the man who was legally, if not actually, her husband; but the irresistible fascination of the subject betrayed her into reciprocating Marian's remarks. And thus, as has been said, though the damp curtains of their bonnets napped smartly into their faces, and their wrappers clung about them to wearisomeness, they lived all this afternoon in memories of green, sunny, romantic Talbothays.

'You can see a gleam of a hill within a few miles o'Froom Valley from here when 'tis fine,' said Marian.

'Ah! Can you?' said Tess, awake to the new value of this locality. So the two forces were at work here as everywhere, the inherent will to enjoy, and the circumstantial will against enjoyment. Marian's will had a method of assisting itself by taking from her pocket as the afternoon wore on a pint bottle corked with white rag, from which she invited Tess to drink. Tess's unassisted power of dreaming, however, being enough for her sublimation at present, she declined except the merest sip, and then Marian took a pull herself from the spirits.

'I've got used to it,' she said, 'and can't leave it off now. 'Tis my only comfort – You see I lost him: you didn't; and you can do without it perhaps.'

Tess thought her loss as great as Marian's, but upheld by the dignity of being Angel's wife, in the letter at least, she accepted Marian's differentiation.

Amid this scene Tess slaved in the morning frosts and in the afternoon rains. When it was not swede-grubbing it was swede-trimming, in which process they sliced off the earth and the fibres with a bill-hook before storing the roots for future use. At this occupation they could shelter themselves by a thatched hurdle if it rained; but if it was frosty even their thick leather gloves could not prevent the frozen masses they handled from biting their fingers. Still Tess hoped. She had a conviction that sooner or later the magnanimity which she persisted in reckoning as a chief ingredient of Clare's character would lead him to rejoin her.

4 The Study of Speech

Introduction

In both parts of the course, that is at both AS and A2 level, you will answer a question on the nature of spontaneous speech. You will also need to be prepared to answer questions on planned speech as a possible area of comparison at either level. The purpose of this section, therefore, is to give you practice in both of these areas by looking at a range of speech situations. Since spontaneous speech will always be tested at both levels, we will start with that.

Spontaneous speech texts

Text 1

This is a man talking about what he does in the evenings, followed by his thoughts on his local football team, Walsall. He comes from the West Midlands. The text has been given order through the use of punctuation. The gaps represent either pauses or parts of his speech that were not used.

I don't go out much, not in the week, you know. I go out one night a week, and if the wife isn't bothered, I won't, you know, I don't bother. Well, the wife and the daughter generally go out together and I stop in, you know, with the lad . . . but er as g . . . the wife and the daughter they've booked up a show what the women have got up or something, eight fifty to see that man who works . . . impersonates a woman . . . what's his name him who impersonates the women on the television . . .

The other night I couldn't get in . . . interested in it about ho . . . homosexuals, you know, and I said to my wife, I says, er, are you coming to bed? Her says, no. I'm going to see the finish of this. I says, all right then, goodnight, and I went up to bed. I mean . . . I'm not, you know, like that . . .

I used to be keen. I used to be a good footballer myself . . . yeh Goodyears and all those, you know, they was high-class teams, I mean you played for the honour then, I mean, you didn't get nothing out of it . . .

No, no, well, er me and the captain of Guest Keens, we had a trial for Walsall and er we came up the one week and they says, come the next week and play again, see, well in the meantime we've got an important match for the works team, cup final, and the captain says, are you going to Walsall? I said no, the works team's more important to me, see. Course we didn't go, and we had a nasty post card off Walsall FC about it, cos we didn't turn up . . .

Well I won the one cup for them really in . . . erm . . . 1948 . . . er we was er winning one-none half time, and the second half I got three goals, and we won four . . . a . . . an theys . . . and they made me go and have the cup, cos, they said, you've won this cup and you're going to have it, and I . . . I . . . present . . . presented with it, you know . . .

I could have done, yes, If I'd have stuck to it, you know, but . . . er . . . well . . . when, you know . . . no, no . . . but I mean, you didn't get a lot then if you played professional, I mean, it was a poor wage then, years ago . . . but it . . . it was an honour to play, they didn't play for the money like they do today . . . well, they've got to make it while they're fit, cos you never know what's going to happen . . .

Well Dave Mackay was on the wireless this morning before I come out, you know, and they was interviewing him, the reporter, and he said he . . . he couldn't understand it why they couldn't score at home . . . I mean, but win away, you know . . . played for Derby, half-back, didn't he? Yes, I do. I always like to see them win, and that, but er . . . something . . . lacking there, definitely . . .

Well Walsall can if they dish the football up. Course they couldn't keep me away years ago. I used to go to every . . . well, I think it's been about six or eight years, when they played Sunderland down here in the cup, and Liverpool . . . I paid a man to do my job, here of a Saturday afternoon to go and see the two matches. And when I come back . . . I was away, say, two hours . . . I'd still got the same work to do . . . nothing had been done . . .

Well er they never spent no money but they got local talent . . . they got a lot of local talent what come up . . . you know, like . . . out of the amateur sides. That's where they go wrong, they don't go to the proper matches . . . er . . . like Shrewsbury, now, Chick Bates, they had him from Stourbridge for about two hundred and fifty pound fee . . . and he's scoring two or three goals a match now . . . I mean Walsall could've done with a man like him.

Points of linguistic interest

◆ the speaker's use of non-standard English
◆ his use of fillers
◆ the way he deals with his subject matter.

Assignment

What features of speech indicate that the speaker is talking spontaneously? How does he convey his feelings about:

◆ the cross-dressing TV star
◆ Walsall FC's performance and his memories of their 'glory days'?

Text 2

In this text a customer, C, asks for advice from a member of staff (S) at the Office of Consumer Affairs. The conversation takes place over the telephone.

S: er yes

C: I want to get your advice on a jacket I bought now the jacket's a hundred and twenty pounds (.) and when I washed it following the instructions the jacket ran now the shop want it back to send it to their lab or whatever (.) what am I entitled to for the jacket (.) they're now half price

S: okay you were returning the jacket to the store

C: yes

S: and what (.) were they accepting responsibility

C: well she said send it in that it was a mess and that they'd send it to whatever department they'd send it to

S: right but they haven't actually accepted that the jacket was faulty at the moment?

C: no no

S: okay well first thing here I'll go through the legislation give you a guideline as to what rights are involved (.) now the act is what's called the sale of goods act

C: yes

S: now that states that when you purchase goods (2.0) those goods should be fit for their purpose (.) of merchantable quality and as described now (.) if a fault develops in the jacket within an unreasonable length of time you have a right to seek redress from the shop

C: yeah

S: now the normal rule is (.) if the fault is minor your rights are to a repair where if the fault is major your rights are to a refund or replacement

C: mmmh yes

S: so what you you should do is contact the store (.) explain your complaint to them and see if you can negotiate one of those solutions

C: yeah

S: either to the repair replacement or refund

C: but what my point is like it's a jacket and white and the red is all gone through the white erm the jacket was a hundred and twenty they're now sixty erm one hundred and nineteen they're now fifty nine whatever so say one hundred and twenty they're now sixty err (1.0) if they give me a new jacket valued at sixty pounds am I entitled to sixty pounds as well

S: what you're generally entitled to would be (.) if they accept that the item is faulty would be to a refund or replacement now if they replace it with an identical jacket

C: yeah

S: and you're willing to accept that

C: mmmh

S: then your rights would generally be to that if you're talking about a refund on the price that you actually er paid for the jacket

C: yes

S: that would be the full refund of money

[

C: yes yes but if I take a halfprice jacket a similar jacket at half price am I still

[

S: if it's a if it's an identical replacement jacket you know
                                                    [
C: yes
S: that's all you would be generally entitled to you know would
                                                    [
C: yes
S: be an identical replacement and that
C: yes
S: because you would be receiving like for like
C: yes that's fair enough that's what I wanted to clarify before I go back into
them no they're they're quite nice about it you know and they'll take the jacket in
which is something
S: yeah
C: you know
S: well it (.) be a matter of discussing that and see will they concede that there
is a fault then in the actual jacket
        [
C: yeah   yeah fair enough thanks for your advice
S: okay
C: okay byebye
            [
S: right ho bye now

Points of linguistic interest

◆ the use of turntaking
◆ questions and answering.

Assignment

How does each of the speakers use language to clarify the situation being discussed? What evidence is there that this conversation is not face-to face?

Text 3

A: does anyone want a chocolate bar or anything
B: oh yeah yes please
                [
C: yes please
B: *(laughs)*
C: *(laughs)*
A: you can have either a Mars Bar, Kit-Kat or erm cherry Bakewell
C: oh erm it's a toss-up between the cherry Bakewell and the Mars Bar isn't it
                                                    [
A: Well shall I
bring some in then cos you might want another one cos I don't want them all,
I'm gonna be

C: miss paranoid about weight aren't you

A: yes but you know

C: you're not fat Mand

A: I will be if I'm not careful

B: oh God

A: I ate almost a whole jar of raisins this weekend *(other 2 laugh)* my Mum gave me all these

      [

C: look at her look

A: she goes oh *(inaudible)*

C: what was that about, you said about you and your Mum don't get on *(B laughs)* I'd say you got on all right with that big wodge of food there

                          [

A: we can relate to chocolate (.) I think they're the little ones actually so you can have one of them and one of them if you like

B: oh those cherry Bakewells look lovely

C: they do don't they

A: oh they were (.) gorgeous (.) did you say you'd like a cup of tea

B: yes

C: all right then

A: sound like a right mother don't I

C: you do

B: but they would go smashing with a cup of tea wouldn't they

A: they would yeah

B: cup of tea and a fag

A: cup of tea and a fag Misses, we're gonna have to move the table I think

C: yeah d'you like Sarah's table she's constructed of erm boots and and a book

A: oh that's brilliant

C: eh that's really good there look

B: and it's got the Milky Way wrapper as that little extra support

C: I like Sunday nights for some reason, I don't know why

B: *(laughs)* cos you come home

C: I come home

B: you come home to us

A: and pig out

B: yeah yeah

C: Sunday's a really nice day I think

B: it certainly is

C: it's a really nice relaxing day

B: it's an earring it's an earring

                    [

C: oh lovely oh lovely

B: it's fallen apart a bit but

C: it's quite a nice one actually (.) I like that I bet (.) is that supposed to be straight

B: yeah

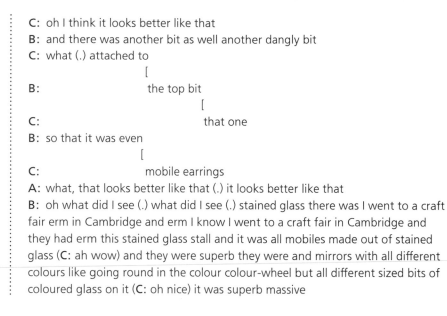

C: oh I think it looks better like that

B: and there was another bit as well another dangly bit

C: what (.) attached to
[

B: the top bit
[

C: that one

B: so that it was even
[

C: mobile earrings

A: what, that looks better like that (.) it looks better like that

B: oh what did I see (.) what did I see (.) stained glass there was I went to a craft fair erm in Cambridge and erm I know I went to a craft fair in Cambridge and they had erm this stained glass stall and it was all mobiles made out of stained glass (**C:** ah wow) and they were superb they were and mirrors with all different colours like going round in the colour colour-wheel but all different sized bits of coloured glass on it (**C:** oh nice) it was superb massive

Points of linguistic interest

◆ topicality and change of subject
◆ informality
◆ use of non-standard English.

Assignment

In what ways do each of the girls make their feelings known about:

◆ overeating and weight problems
◆ life's little luxuries
◆ the craft fair at Cambridge?

The following conversations are spoken between two people over the telephone (Text 4) and between three people face-to-face (Text 5).

Text 4

S: hello hello Telephone Companions can I help you

F: er good evening love I phoned you (.) Friday night er Wednesday

S: Wednesday night yes

F: about me boyfriend

S: oh yes

F: well I couldn't get him to phone you that night

S: I see

F: so anyway I'm just meeting him now

S: yes

F: shall I get him to phone you?

S: yes alright dear

F: is it alright
S: yes it'll be alright dear just wait a minute
F: pardon co *(inaudible)*
                    [
S: what's your na what's your name please love
F: his name's Arthur Jones
S: wha what's yours though your first name love
F: er Felicity
S: Felicity (.) okay who did you speak to
F: pardon
S: who did you speak to on Wednesday night *(inaudible)* remember?
F: oh well he's always on about committing suicide you know
S: oh yeh-y-your boyfriend is (.) I see
F: yeah
S: okay

Text 5

A: Hi. I've got one. It took ages.
B: Hi. Mind all that stuff.
A: You've got a lot done.
B: Colin's given us a hand.
A: Hi.
C: Hi.
B: Where'd you get it?
A: Holroyd's.
B: Give us it here.
C: Is this coming out?
B: What? Er (.) no (.) leave that (.) thanks.
A: Is it right?
B: Yes.
C: What needs doing next?
B: Let's knock off for a brew.
C: Great idea.
A: Look I'm a bit pushed, I'll come back this aft. Gavin and Simon'll help.
B: Keep out of the boozer.
A: Skint anyway.
C: It's nearly off, this.
B: It'll plaster back in again. Don't make it worse.

Points of linguistic interest

◆ adjacency pairings and chaining
◆ deictic expression.

Assignment

In what ways do these two interactions differ? Who is in charge in each exchange? Use evidence from each text to back up your answer.

Planned speech

Text 6

Earl Spencer gave this address at the funeral of his sister, Diana Princess of Wales. It was televised live to millions of people around the world. This is an extract from the funeral oration.

I stand before you today the representative of a family in grief, in a country in mourning, before a world in shock. We are all united, not only in our desire to pay our respects to Diana, but rather in our need to do so.

For such was her extraordinary appeal that the tens of millions of people taking part in this service all over the world via television and radio who never actually met her, feel that they, too, lost someone close to them in the early hours of Sunday morning. It is a more remarkable tribute to Diana than I can ever hope to offer her today.

Diana was the very essence of compassion, of duty, of style, of beauty. All over the world she was a symbol of selfless humanity. All over the world, a standard bearer for the rights of the truly downtrodden, a very British girl who transcended nationality. Someone with a natural nobility who was classless and who proved in the last year that she needed no royal title to continue to generate her particular brand of magic.

Today is our chance to say thank you for the way you brightened our lives, even though God granted you but half a life. We will all feel cheated always that you were taken from us so young, and yet we must learn to be grateful that you came along at all. Only now that you are gone do we truly appreciate what we are now without and we want you to know that life without you is very, very difficult.

We have all despaired at our loss over the past week and only the strength of the message you gave us through your years of giving has afforded us the strength to move forward.

There is a temptation to rush to canonise your memory, there is no need to do so. You stand tall enough as a human being of unique qualities not to be seen as a saint. Indeed, to sanctify your memory would be to miss out on the very core of your being, your wonderfully mischievous sense of humour with a laugh that bent you double.

Your joy for life, transmitted wherever you took your smile, and the sparkle in those unforgettable eyes. Your boundless energy, which you could barely contain.

But your greatest gift was your intuition and it was a gift you used wisely. This is what underpinned all your other wonderful attributes and if we look to analyse what it was about you that had such a wide appeal we find it in your instinctive feel for what was really important in all our lives.

Without your God-given sensitivity we would be immersed in greater ignorance at the anguish of Aids and HIV sufferers, the plight of the homeless, the isolation of lepers, the random destruction of landmines.

Diana explained to me once that it was her innermost feelings of suffering that made it possible for her to connect with her constituency of the rejected. And here we come to another truth about her. For all the status, the glamour, the applause, Diana remained throughout a very insecure person at heart, almost childlike in her desire to do good for others so she could release herself from deep feelings of unworthiness of which her eating disorders were merely a symptom.

The world sensed this part of her character and cherished her for her vulnerability whilst admiring her for her honesty.

The last time I saw Diana was on July 1, her birthday, in London, when typically she was not taking time to celebrate her special day with friends but was guest of honour at a special charity fundraising evening. She sparkled, of course, but I would rather cherish the days I spent with her in March when she came to visit me and my children in our home in South Africa. I am proud of the fact apart from when she was on display meeting President Mandela we managed to contrive to stop the ever-present paparazzi from getting a single picture of her – that meant a lot to her.

These were days I will always treasure.

Earl Spencer giving the address at his sister's funeral in Westminster Abbey

Points of linguistic interest

◆ use of pronominative form
◆ use of rhetorical features.

Assignment

In what ways does the speaker communicate his feelings in this extract? How does he reinforce his ideas?

Text 7

General George S. Patton gave this speech on May 17, 1944. In the speech he addresses his troops shortly before the invasion of Normandy, speaking of their courage and dedication in a very forthright manner.

Men, this stuff some sources sling around about America wanting to stay out of the war and not wanting to fight is a lot of baloney! Americans love to fight, traditionally. All real Americans love the sting and clash of battle. America loves a winner. America will not tolerate a loser. Americans despise a coward; Americans play to win. That's why America has never lost and never will lose a war.

You are not all going to die. Only two percent of you, right here today, would be killed in a major battle.

Death must not be feared. Death, in time, comes to all of us. And every man is scared in his first action. If he says he's not, he's a goddamn liar. Some men are cowards, yes, but they fight just the same, or get the hell slammed out of them.

The real hero is the man who fights even though he's scared. Some get over their fright in a minute, under fire; others take an hour; for some it takes days; but a real man will never let the fear of death overpower his honour, his sense of duty, to his country and to his manhood.

All through your Army careers, you've been bitching about what you call 'chicken-shit drills'. That, like everything else in the Army, has a definite purpose. That purpose is instant obedience to orders and to create and maintain constant alertness! This must be bred into every soldier. A man must be alert all the time if he expects to stay alive. If not, some German son-of-a-bitch will sneak up behind him with a sock full of shit! There are four hundred neatly marked graves somewhere in Sicily, all because one man went to sleep on his job: but they are German graves, because we caught the bastards asleep!

An Army is a team, lives, sleeps, fights, and eats as a team. This individual hero stuff is a lot of horseshit! The bilious bastards who write that kind of stuff for the Saturday Evening Post don't know any more about real fighting under fire than they know about fucking! Every single man in the Army plays a vital role. Every man has his job to do and must do it. What if every truck driver decided that he didn't like the whine of a shell overhead, turned yellow and jumped headlong into a ditch? What if every man thought, 'They won't miss me, just one in millions'? Where in Hell would we be now? Where would our country, our loved ones, our homes, even the world, be?

No, thank God, Americans don't think like that. Every man does his job, serves the whole. Ordnance men supply and maintain the guns and vast machinery of this war, to keep us rolling. Quartermasters bring up clothes and food, for where we're going, there isn't a hell of a lot to steal. Every last man on K.P. has a job to do, even the guy who boils the water to keep us from getting the G.I. shits!

. . . We want to get this thing over and get the hell out of here, and get at those purple-pissin' Japs!!! The shortest road home is through Berlin and Tokyo! We'll win this war, but we'll win it only by showing the enemy we have more guts than they have or ever will have!

There's one great thing you men can say when it's all over and you're home once more. You can thank God that twenty years from now, when you're sitting around the fireside with your grandson on your knee and he asks you what you did in the war, you won't have to shift him to the other knee, cough, and say, 'I shovelled shit in Louisiana'.

Points of linguistic interest

◆ the use of demotic language
◆ the aggression and overt masculinity of the speech.

Assignment

In what ways does Patton express his true feelings when speaking to the troops? How does Patton whip up patriotic fervour in this speech? How do you think the troops would react to this speech?

The leaders of the two main political parties in Britain at their respective party conferences gave the following two speeches in 1998. Tony Blair's is Text 8; William Hague's is Text 9.

Text 8

Today I want to set an ambitious course for this country: to be nothing less than the model 21st century nation, a beacon to the world. It means drawing deep into the richness of the British character. Creative. Compassionate. Outward-looking. Old British values, but a new British confidence.

We can never be the biggest. We may never again be the mightiest. But we can be the best. The best place to live. The best place to bring up children, the best place to lead a fulfilled life, the best place to grow old.

And we cannot say we want a strong and secure society when we ignore its very foundation: family life. This is not about preaching to individuals about their private lives. It is addressing a huge social problem. Attitudes have changed. The world has changed. But I am a modern man leading a modern country and this is a modern crisis. Nearly 100,000 teenage pregnancies every year. Elderly parents with whom families cannot cope. Children growing up without role models they can respect and learn from. More and deeper poverty. More crime. More truancy. More neglect of educational opportunities. And above all, more unhappiness. That unhappiness must change.

I give you this pledge. Every area of this Government's policy will be scrutinised to see how it affects family life. Every policy examined, every initiative tested, every avenue explored to see how we strengthen our families, and you will have a ministerial group to drive it through.

And let me tell you this directly. Yes, we are new Labour. Yes, our policies and attitudes have changed. But there are no old Labour or new Labour values. There are Labour values. They are what make us the party of compassion; of social justice; of the struggle against poverty and inequality; of liberty; of basic human solidarity; and the day we cease to be those things is the day we keep the name of the Labour Party but lose the reason for its existence.

Today, I issue a challenge to you. Help us make Britain that beacon shining throughout the world. Unite behind our mission to modernise our country for all our people. For there is a place for all the people in new Britain, and there is a role for all the people in its creation. Believe in us as much as we believe in you.

Text 9

Today I'd like to talk about my kind of Conservatism, the party I lead, the things I believe in.

I'd like to tell you about an open Conservatism that is tolerant, that believes freedom is about much more than economics, that believes freedom doesn't stop at the shop counter. I'd like to tell you about a democratic, popular Conservatism that listens, that has compassion at its core.

I want to tell you about a Conservatism rooted in its traditions, but embracing the future. I want to tell you about a changing Conservatism that acknowledges its mistakes. But I also want to tell you about a proud Conservatism that has served this nation well and will do so again.

We won't just be a party of power, we will be a party of principle, too. In the coming years we'll be the only party of principle in this country.

I'm going to tell you what I believe in. First of all, I believe in freedom. In Thomas Jefferson's famous words, 'the price of liberty is eternal vigilance'. Two hundred years later we've got to be vigilant against a Government whose every instinct is to boss, to meddle, to interfere and to control. We are the only party in Britain which believes in freedom as a birthright to be protected rather than a concession to be handed down. So I believe in freedom.

So I believe in a Europe of nation states. So I believe in freedom. I believe in enterprise. I believe in education. I believe in self-reliance. I believe in obligation to others. I believe in the nation.

So let's hold our heads high and say to new Labour and the whole world: these are the things we believe in, these are the values from which we will never retreat. Let's say to the world, this is what we believe in and this is what we will always stand for.

Let's challenge new Labour: this is what we believe, what do you believe? These are our values, where are yours? This is what is sacred to us, when will anything be sacred to you? Some people think none of this matters any more. They think we've no more need for beliefs. We've reached the end of history. The battle's been won, the game is over, the fat lady has sung. But I'm here to tell you they're wrong. Our beliefs and our values matter now more than ever.

Points of linguistic interest

◆ the use of concrete and abstract ideas
◆ the use of part sentences and sound bites.

Assignment

Compare the two speeches, showing which you feel to be the most effective in terms of the message being conveyed and the method of its delivery.

Examination assignment

Read the following transcription of a conversation between two people. How does each of the participants use speech in this exchange? In your answer you should show

◆ who is in charge and what evidence there is to show this
◆ how the speakers use certain features to help the conversation move forward.

Transcription key: (.)   Micropause
                        (1.0)   Pause in seconds
                        ::   elongation of sound
                        [overlap

A: Erm (.) I seem to be (.) a bit los::t I'm trying to get to Yor::k
B: Oh (.) oh well that's quite straight for::ward from here (.) if you just carry on:: down this road this is Heslington Lane:: (.) just
                                                    [
A: Yeah
B: carry on straight ahead:: (.) the road
                              [
A: Yeah
B: forks to the left but (.) ignore that just go straight ahead:: (.) and that's Broa::dway (0.5) when you come to the end of Broadway there are a set of traffic lights::
A: Ye::s how far's that
B: Oh:: (0.5) mile (.) probably
A: Go straight ahead for a mile
B: Yes::
A: Ignore:: the left fork
                   [
B: Ignore the left for::k
A: Yeah (.) then I get to some traffic lights
B: You get to some traffic lights (.) turn right at the traffic lights:: (.) carry

```
                                                              [
A:                                                            huhuh
B:  on down there that's the main:: road into Yor::k (.) just sort of carry on
down there you'll come to some traffic lights:: keep in the right hand lane (.) and
                                                              [
A:                                                            Yeah
B:  there are some traffic lights::
                      [
B:                    What is it a dual carriageway then
A:  Yes it's a dual carriageway (.) part of the way anyway
A:  OK
B:  If you carry er keep on in the right hand lane:: (.) you
                                          [
A:                                        Yeah
B:  come to some more traffic lights there's a roundabout there:: you'll see (.)
erm (.) Clifford's Tower on the right::
A:  Wha (.) what's:: Clifford's Tower
B:  Yes it's a big tower on a mou::nd (.) you'll be actually:: alongsi on the road
alongside (0.5) Clifford's Tower (.) You're in York then
                          [
A:                        Ok::
B:  There's also by Clifford's Tower there's a (.) car park you can park there and then::
A:  OK so I look out for:: a tower on top of a mound and head towards that:: (.)
                                  [           [
B:                                Yes         Yes
```

Student response

> The situation in which this conversation is carried out determines its
> format and content. Because the relationship between the two
> participants is unfamiliar and formal, the way they speak and the things
> they communicate are vitally important.
>
> The two participants have different roles in this exchange; in its most
> uncomplicated definition, A provides questions and B provides answers,
> since the former wants directions and the latter is in a position to give
> them. A commences the exchange, with the introduction, 'Erm (.) I seem
> to be (.) a bit los::t . . .' The hesitations and beginning filler suggest that
> A does not want to go straight to the subject, because he feels some kind
> of explanation and modesty is necessary. The elongation of the final word
> of his utterance 'los::t' indicates that his turn is being relinquished as well
> as showing his unfortunate situation and thus pleading to the better
> nature of A.
>
> However, after this point, it is B who is in charge for most of the
>
> →

conversation. This can be seen from the amount of speech which each participant has. B provides a long and detailed answer to the initial request, giving five statements with only minimal feedback from A. B's statements include lots of detail, probably more than A would be able to remember, about place names, which are fairly insignificant. An example of this is the confusion over 'Clifford's Tower', which means nothing to A '. . . what's:: Clifford's Tower'. B's information here was clearly a hindrance and A seeks elucidation. A's responses are generally kept to short utterances or direct questions such as, 'Ye::s how far's that', and back channelling which is designed to encourage responses.

B frequently uses elongated sounds in his speech, normally suggesting the end of a turn of speaking, such as in B's utterance, '. . . there are a set of traffic lights::' This is the end of the utterance. However, B often carries on either because of encouragement from A in the form of back channel behaviour or because the pauses and elongated sounds are to allow time to think. Quite unusually, B uses elongated sounds to fill pauses rather than fillers such as 'erm.' For example, B uses an elongated sound before a micro-pause in the utterance, 'If you carry er keep on in the right hand lane::(.) you'. This is also one of the few utterances in which B uses a filler to hold the turn.

Because B is required to give directions and answers, the information takes the form of commands and imperative verbs. For example, B often begins his utterances with commands such as 'Go' 'Ignore,' or 'Carry on.' These make the statements clear as well as reflecting B's dominant role.

Back channel behaviour is an important feature of keeping a conversation going. A speaker who feels that he or she is being responded to is more likely to continue speaking. A exhibits a large amount of back channel behaviour in this conversation. Agreement and feedback such as 'Yeah' and 'OK' encourage B to continue speaking and giving information which A requires. This feedback often occurs during a pause in B's speech. B gives much less feedback, principally because he does the main bulk of the speaking. However, he encourages A's final utterance with two 'Yes.' These may either be to confirm A's understanding, or, because they are very close together, to hurry A's speech or try to regain the turn.

Fuller feedback from both speakers also helps the conversation to move forward. A often verifies and confirms what B has told him, by repeating in his own words B's instructions. For example, A turns B's utterance, 'forks to the left but (.) ignore that . . .' into 'Ignore:: the left fork.' This feedback and affirmation is typical for the situation of giving directions.

Questions help to spark off developments in the conversation, allowing it to move forward. A is able to get the more specific information which he wants from B by asking questions such as '. . . how far's that' and '. . . is it a dual carriageway . . .' These questions elicit a response from B,

→

but they do not cause significant topic changes. Indeed, the topicality does not change since the primary purpose of the exchange is to elicit directions. Because of this, B continues eagerly giving information, perhaps a little too eagerly and in too much detail. B occasionally breaks Grice's maxims of relevance and quantity in saying too much information which may be unnecessary. For instance, he mentions place names such as 'Broadway,' which are not relevant for A, who will not know these; perhaps B simply gives them as points of reference.

In the opening utterance, A, instead of asking a direct question, implies his desire for information with a statement '. . . I'm trying to get to Yor::k'. This confirms the relative formality of the situation. A perhaps considers it impolite to be direct in his question, or perhaps is a little embarrassed at being lost. At various points, however, A takes control of the conversation by confirming what B has told him. For instance, A finally reduces B's instructions to a bare minimum in the utterance, 'OK so I look out for:: a tower on top of a mound and head towards that::'. A seems to be trying to end the conversation, which has probably been longer and more detailed than expected but also wants to clarify the instructions that have been given. Before this, B has tried to hold the turn by leaving his previous utterance unfinished and with an elongated sound on the last word. The utterance ends with '. . . you can park there and then::'. A interrupts before B finishes his utterance and successfully takes the turn from A, but this is perhaps the only point in the conversation where A is notionally in charge.

There is presumably a closing sequence in this exchange since the two speakers have established a rapport and would say goodbye to each other, if only out of politeness. Because of the detail of B's answers, it is perhaps A who instigates the ending. ◆

Examiner's comments

This has all the hallmarks of a successful answer. It answers both parts of the question in a logical and structured fashion, employing an effective framework for analysis which helps the student make the answer coherent and ensures coverage of all aspects of the question.

The student also uses relevant terminology in an unforced manner, which illustrates the necessity of learning which tools to use from the literary and linguistic toolkit, as well as highlighting the need to know how to use these tools effectively. The terminology is used as a way of answering the question on how each speaker uses language, thus focusing entirely on the question. There are plenty of detailed examples that are discussed throughout the essay, and the conclusion is conceptualized by predicting the outcome of the exchange. A first-rate answer.

5 Comparative Literary Studies

Introduction

The fourth unit of the A Level course (the first unit of A2) is entitled 'Comparative Literary Studies'. This unit involves the detailed study of one pair of texts from the pairings offered in the syllabus.

In this section of the book you will be given a variety of questions on different texts, using extracts as starting points. In the exam, the questions will not include extracts because you will have the texts with you – you will be referred to specific passages or sections. With this proviso, the questions given here are of the kind that you could expect to meet in the exam. If you have not studied the texts referred to in a question, use the passages as practice in looking at the different ways writers use language – they are self-contained pieces. If you have studied the text, however, you will find further questions will enable you to practise the kinds of tasks that you are likely to face in the exam.

In order to tackle the questions it is a good idea to have a method of approaching your study of a prose text. This unit focuses on the ways in which language is used in pairs of texts, and so **purpose** and **audience** are key issues. The following outline is one way of tackling the variety of question types that could be asked when comparing set texts.

Frameworks

◆ Identify comparative areas and issues in the texts

Analysis and explanation

◆ Identify, exemplify and explain the central features of the texts, using contextual and structural frameworks
◆ Describe and compare the features of the text, e.g. exploration of ideas, themes, characters, linguistic issues
◆ Consider and compare the meanings and effects created in each text
◆ Consider different levels of analysis.

Evaluation

◆ Consider and evaluate particular aspects of the texts with reference to explanatory frameworks.

The specification offers the following advice:

◆ Candidates should be prepared to comment on specific sections of the text and widen their comments to the whole of both texts, with reference to the way language is used.

◆ Candidates should be prepared to answer on thematic, generic, development and stylistic links and comparisons in texts.

◆ Candidates may be asked how literary issues are raised by the writer.

In drawing comparisons between texts, there is a range of relevant features that you should focus on. These include comparison of:

◆ character presentation
◆ thematic presentation
◆ presentation of setting and atmosphere
◆ narrative viewpoint
◆ semantic features
◆ phonological features
◆ grammar
◆ structure
◆ lexis.

We will begin by looking at an extract from *Talking Heads 2* by Alan Bennett (Text 1) and an extract from *The Miller's Tale* by Geoffrey Chaucer (Text 2).

Text 1

TALKING HEADS 2

Afternoon. The kitchen. Against a blank, wallpapered wall. One chair. Possibly some artificial flowers. Similar settings throughout.

I'd be the same if it was a cat. Because they make as much mess as dogs. Only cats you can be allergic to, so people make allowances. And flowers, of course, some people. Only we don't have flowers. Well, we do but they're all washable. I just think it spies on me, that tongue lolling out.

He took the van over to Rawdon last night. Said it was Rawdon anyway. Doing something or other, fly-tipping probably. Takes Tina which was a relief from the woof-woofing plus it gave me a chance to swill.

I'd had Mrs Catchpole opposite banging on the door in the afternoon saying she was going to the council because it wanted putting down. I said, 'I agree.' She said, 'I'm getting a petition up.' I said, 'Well, when you do, fetch it across because I'll be the first signatory.' I hate the flaming dog. Of course she doesn't do it with him. Never makes a muff when he's around.

He comes in after midnight, puts his clothes in the washer. I said to him last week, 'Why don't you do your washing at a cultivated hour?' He said, 'You're lucky I do it at all.' Still, at least the washer's in the shed. I shouted down, 'That dogs not inside is she?' He said, 'No. Get to sleep.' Which I was doing only when he comes up he has nothing on. He leaves it a bit then slides over to my side and starts carrying on.

Found a dog hair or two on the carpet this morning so that meant another shampooing job. I only did it last week. This shampoo's got air-freshener in, plus a disinfectant apparently.

Non-stop down at the yard since they started killing off the cows, so when he comes in this dinner-time he wants to eat straight off. Swills his boots under the outside tap and he's coming in like that. I said, 'Stuart. You know the rules. Take them off.' He said, 'There's no time.' So I said, 'Well, if there's not time you'll have it on the step.' Sits there eating and feeding Tina. She licks his boots. Literally. I suppose it's with him coming straight from the slaughterhouse. Seems to have lost another anorak, this one fur-lined.

FADE

She comes up this afternoon, his mother, all dolled up. Says, 'You've got this nice place. How do you manage with our Stuart?' I said, 'I've got him trained.' She said 'He's not trained when he comes down our house.' 'Well,' I said, 'perhaps he doesn't get the encouragement.' She said, 'I don't like it when they're too tidy. It's not natural.'

Not natural at their house. They've no culture at all. First time I went down there they were having their dinner and there was a pan stuck on the table. When it comes to evolution they're scarcely above pig-sty level. And she must be sixty, still dyes her hair, fag in her mouth, big ear-rings. She said, 'You don't mind if I smoke? Or do you want me to sit on the step?'

I gave her a saucer only it didn't do much good, ash all over the shop. She does it on purpose. It had gone five, she said, 'Where is he?' I said, 'Where he generally is at this time of day: slitting some defenceless creature's throat. They're on overtime.'

She went before it got dark. Said she was nervous what with this roller on the loose. Made a fuss of Tina. Remembered her when she was a puppy running round their house. I remember it an' all. Doing its business all up and down, the place stank. It was me that trained Stuart. Me that trained the dog.

Except for the din. Can't train that. Leaves off, of course when he appears. He doesn't believe she does it. I said to him, 'Is it safe for me to go on to the library?' He said, 'Why?' I said, 'There's a lass dead in Wakefield now.' He said, 'You don't cross any waste ground. Take Tina.'

Anyway I didn't go and when he's changed out of his muck and swilled everything off he put on his navy shirt, little chain round his neck and the tan slacks we bought him in Marbella. I brought him a beer in a glass while I had a sherry. Him sat on one side of the fire, me on the other, watching TV with the sound down. I said, 'This is a nice civilised evening.'

Except of course madam gets wind of the fact that we're having a nice time and starts whimpering and whatnot and jumping up outside the window and carries on and carries on until he has to take her out. Gone two hours so I was in bed when he got back.

Comes upstairs without his trousers on. I said, 'What've you done with your slacks?' He said, 'The dog jumped up and got mud on. Anyway it's quite handy isn't it?' I said, 'Why?' He said, 'Why do you think? Move up.'

Lots of shouting and whatnot. I thought in the middle of it, it's a blessing

we're detached. 'Sorry about that,' he said when he'd done. 'I get carried away.'
Loudspeaker van came round this afternoon saying the police were going to be
coming round. House to house. I was just getting some stuff ready to take to the
dry cleaners while it was light still.

Couldn't find his slacks.

FADE

Text 2

THE MILLER'S TALE

Heere bigynneth the Millere his tale.

> Whilom ther was dwellynge at Oxenford
> A riche gnof, that gestes heeld to bord,
> And of his craft he was a carpenter.
> With hym ther was dwellynge a poure scoler,
> Hadde lerned art, but al his fantasye
> Was turned for to lerne astrologye,
> And koude a certeyn of conclusiouns,
> To demen by interrogaciouns,
> If that men asked hym, in certein houres
> Whan that men sholde have droghte or elles shoures,
> Or if men asked hym what sholde bifalle
> Of every thyng; I may nat rekene hem alle.
> This clerk was cleped hende Nicholas.
> Of deerne love he koude and of solas;
> And therto he was sleigh and ful privee,
> And lyk a mayden meke for to see.
> A chambre hadde he in that hostelrye
> Allone, withouten any compaignye,
> Ful fetisly ydight with herbes swoote;
> And he hymself as sweete as is the roote
> Of lycorys or any cetewale.
> His Almageste, and bookes grete and smale,
> His astrelabie, longynge for his art,
> His augrym stones layen faire apart,
> On shelves couched at his beddes heed;
> His presse ycovered with a faldyng reed;
> And al above ther lay a gay sautrie,
> On which he made a-nyghtes melodie
> So swetely that all the chambre rong;
> And *Angelus ad virginem* he song;
> And after that he song the Kynges Noote.
> Ful often blessed was his myrie throte.
> And thus this sweete clerk his tyme spente
> After his freendes fyndyng and his rente.

Analytical tasks

1 For each text, make notes on:
   a) what is happening in the passage
   b) what kind of tone the writer creates
   c) the techniques the writer uses to create this tone.

2 Write an essay in which you compare and contrast the techniques used by each writer to achieve his desired effects and evaluate the success of each technique.

Points of linguistic interest

Text 1

◆ the monologue approach
◆ the use of direct speech
◆ the use of irony
◆ the description through hints and innnuendo.

Text 2

◆ the leisurely opening
◆ the descriptions of characters
◆ details of fourteenth century life
◆ association of Nicholas with secrecy, love, and music.

Assignment

Choose one extract from *The Miller's Tale* and one extract from *Talking Heads 2* which you have found amusing. Examine the ways in which the writer creates humour in each extract and comment on the effectiveness of the techniques used.

The following passages are both taken from the early parts of novels. Text 3 is from *Snow Falling on Cedars* by David Guterson and the Text 4 is from *The Shipping News* by E. Annie Proulx.

Text 3

SNOW FALLING ON CEDARS

The accused man, Kabuo Miyamoto, sat proudly upright with a rigid grace, his palms placed softly on the defendant's table – the posture of a man who has detached himself insofar as this is possible at his own trial. Some in the gallery would later say that his stillness suggested a disdain for the proceedings; others felt certain it veiled a fear of the verdict that was to come. Whichever it was, Kabuo showed nothing – not even a flicker of the eyes. He was dressed in a white shirt worn buttoned to the throat and gray, neatly pressed trousers. His figure, especially the neck and shoulders, communicated the impression of irrefutable physical strength and of precise, even imperial bearing. Kabuo's features were smooth and angular; his hair had been cropped close to his skull in a manner that made its musculature prominent. In the face of the charge that had been leveled against him he sat with his dark eyes trained straight ahead and did not appear moved at all.

In the public gallery every seat had been taken, yet the court-room suggested nothing of the carnival atmosphere sometimes found at country murder trials. In fact, the eighty-five citizens gathered there seemed strangely subdued and contemplative. Most of them had known Carl Heine, a salmon gill-netter with a wife and three children, who was buried now in the Lutheran cemetery up on Indian Knob Hill. Most had dressed with the same communal propriety they felt on Sundays before attending church services, and since the courtroom, however stark, mirrored in their hearts the dignity of their prayer houses, they conducted themselves with churchgoing solemnity.

This courtroom, Judge Llewellyn Fielding's, down at the end of a damp, drafty hallway on the third floor of the Island County Courthouse, was run-down and small as courtrooms go. It was a place of gray-hued and bleak simplicity – a cramped gallery, a bench for the judge, a witness stand, a plywood platform for the jurors, and scuffed tables for the defendant and his prosecutor. The jurors sat with studiously impassive faces as they strained to make sense of matters. The men – two truck farmers, a retired crabber, a bookkeeper, a carpenter, a boat builder, a grocer, and a halibut schooner deckhand – were all dressed in coats and neckties. The women all wore Sunday dresses – a retired waitress, a sawmill secretary, two nervous fisher wives. A hairdresser accompanied them as alternate.

The bailiff, Ed Soames, at the request of Judge Fielding, had given a good head of steam to the sluggish radiators, which now and again sighed in the four corners of the room. In the heat they produced – a humid, overbearing swelter – the smell of sour mildew seemed to rise from everything.

Snow fell that morning outside the courthouse windows, four tall, narrow arches of leaded glass that yielded a great quantity of weak December light. A wind from the sea lofted snowflakes against the windowpanes, where they melted and ran toward the casements. Beyond the courthouse the town of Amity Harbor spread along the island shoreline. A few wind-whipped and decrepit Victorian mansions, remnants of a lost era of seagoing optimism, loomed out of the snowfall on the town's sporadic hills. Beyond them, cedars wove a steep mat of still green. The snow blurred from vision the clean contours of these cedar hills. The sea wind drove snowflakes steadily inland, hurling them against the fragrant trees, and the snow began to settle on the highest branches with a gentle implacability.

The accused man, with one segment of his consciousness, watched the falling snow outside the windows. He had been exiled in the county jail for seventy-seven days – the last part of September, all of October and all of November, the first week of December in jail. There was no window anywhere in his basement cell, no portal through which the autumn light could come to him. He had missed autumn, he realized now – it had passed already, evaporated. The snowfall, which he witnessed out of the corners of his eyes – furious, wind-whipped flakes against the windows – struck him as infinitely beautiful.

Text 4

THE SHIPPING NEWS

Quoyle and Partridge met at a laundromat in Mockingburg, New York. Quoyle was humped over the newspaper, circling help-wanted ads while his Big Man shirts revolved. Partridge remarked that the job market was tight. Yes, said Quoyle, it was. Partridge floated an opinion on the drought, Quoyle nodded. Partridge moved the conversation to the closing of the sauerkraut factory. Quoyle fumbled his shirts from the dryer; they fell on the floor in a rain of hot coins and ballpoint pens. The shirts were streaked with ink. 'Ruined,' said Quoyle.

'Naw,' said Partridge. 'Rub the ink with hot salt and talcum powder. Then wash them again, put a cup of bleach in.'

Quoyle said he would try it. His voice wavered. Partridge was astonished to see the heavy man's colorless eyes enlarged with tears. For Quoyle was a failure at loneliness, yearned to be gregarious, to know his company was a pleasure to others. The dryers groaned.

'Hey, come by some night,' said Partridge, writing his slanting address and phone number on the back of a creased cash register receipt. He didn't have that many friends either.

The next evening Quoyle was there, gripping paper bags. The front of Partridge's house, the empty street drenched in amber light. A gilded hour. In the bags a packet of imported Swedish crackers, bottles of red, pink and white wine, foil-wrapped triangles of foreign cheeses. Some kind of hot, juggling music on the other side of Partridge's door that thrilled Quoyle.

They were friends for a while, Quoyle, Partridge and Mercalia. Their differences: Partridge black, small, a restless traveler across the slope of life, an all-night talker; Mercalia, second wife of Partridge and the color of a brown feather on dark water, a hot intelligence; Quoyle large, white, stumbling along, going nowhere. Partridge saw beyond the present, got quick shots of coming events as though loose brain wires briefly connected. He had been born with a caul; at three, witnessed ball lightning bouncing down a fire escape; dreamed of cucumbers the night before his brother-in-law was stung by hornets. He was sure of his own good fortune. He could blow perfect smoke rings. Cedar waxwings always stopped in his yard on their migration flights.

Now, in the backyard, seeing Quoyle like a dog dressed in a man's suit for a comic photo, Partridge thought of something.

'Ed Punch, managing editor down at the paper where I work is looking for a cheap reporter. Summer's over and his college rats go back to their holes. The paper's junk, but maybe give it a few months, look around for something better. What the hell, maybe you'd like it, being a reporter.'

Quoyle nodded, hand over chin. If Partridge suggested he leap from a bridge he would at least lean on the rail. The advice of a friend.

'Mercalia! I'm saving the heel for you, lovely girl. It's the best part. Come on out here.'

Mercalia put the cap on her pen. Weary of writing of prodigies who bit their hands and gyred around parlor chairs spouting impossible sums, dust rising from the oriental carpets beneath their stamping feet.

Ed Punch talked out of the middle of his mouth. While he talked he examined Quoyle, noticed the cheap tweed jacket the size of a horse blanket, fingernails that looked regularly held to a grindstone. He smelled submission in Quoyle, guessed he was butter of fair spreading consistency.

Quoyle's own eyes roved to a water-stained engraving on the wall. He saw a grainy face, eyes like glass eggs, a fringe of hairs rising from under the collar and cascading over its starched rim. Was it Punch's grandfather in the chipped frame? He wondered about ancestors.

'This is a family paper. We run upbeat stories with a community slant.' The *Mockingburg Record* specialized in fawning anecdotes of local business people, profiles of folksy characters; this thin stuff padded with puzzles and contests, syndicated columns, features and cartoons. There was always a self-help quiz — 'Are You a Breakfast Alcoholic?'

Punch sighed, feigned a weighty decision. 'Put you on the municipal beat to help out Al Catalog. He'll break you in. Get your assignments from him.'

The salary was pathetic, but Quoyle didn't know.

Analytical tasks

1 What do each of these openings describe?

2 What similarities and what differences do you note of the ways in which each writer uses language?

3 Examine each writer's choice of vocabulary and use of description.

4 Write an essay in which you compare and contrast these two extracts and evaluate their success in capturing the reader's attention.

Points of linguistic interest

◆ the use of descriptive language (particularly adjectival choice) to create scene and character
◆ the use of imagery
◆ the syntax and its effects
◆ the choice of vocabulary.

Assignment

Compare the ways in which each writer uses language to create a sense

> of place in *Snow Falling On Cedars* and *The Shipping News*. You should comment on each writer's use of vocabulary, syntax and style in your answer.

The following two extracts are from the play *Murmuring Judges* by David Hare and *Measure for Measure* by William Shakespeare. Each extract shows the ending of the play.

Text 5

MURMURING JUDGES

Woody: Yeah, they'd delivered the brief. A bloke came running round, he said, 'Have you actually got it?' I held it up, I said, 'It's in my hand . . .' He said, 'Oh God, don't tell me . . . That's forty thousand plus fifteen hundred a day.' I said, 'Yes, plus secretarial, this sort of case, don't forget, I don't have to tell you, you'll find the duplicator's running all night.' He looked at me, he said, 'Have you actually got it? In that very envelope?' He said, 'Where do you live? Have you got a garage? Do you need a new loft? What do you drive? Have you got a Jaguar?' What could I say? 'I've got a Jaguar. And I like to see Sir Peter do well.' I said, 'What can I say? You know, you delivered the brief, I hate to have to tell you, it's the custom we have. Once it's in hand, sorry, mate, more than my life's worth, once you put it in hand, you have to come through. Also, you know, there's another thing, I mean, look at it my way . . .' (*Simultaneously with:*)

Barry: . . . but here it's like they're saying, oh no, you know it's no good. You think, oh, if they spent half the time trying to support the actual coppers, I mean getting behind us and helping to get on with the job, if they spent half the time they do thinking up ways of not paying us, then, God knows, we'd all be much better off. Because, I tell you, there isn't a system devised, not one, not one that is conceived in the human brain that any self-respecting copper isn't going to see as a challenge and think, OK, right now, how do I get round it this time? Now look, I mean, for instance, this clothing allowance, I looked this up, look, the question of professional clothing, what you have to wear on undercover work, I mean, I can't walk into a place in my new Armani, or else my cover's blown before I even start. (*Simultaneously with:*)

Irina: First of these is Toby Ellington, who you will all know, who's sent a message saying, yes, this is exactly the kind of action that's needed in the legal profession, how pleased he is, and how, you know, if it were any other day, but he's of course defending in the Irish case; card here also from Lord Bethredge, who's thrilled at the idea. Also, I'm pleased to say we've had some cheques, which is excellent, from Larry Solto, of course, Jim Hail. Mary Handsworth. Basil Hart. All saying, yes, this is exactly the pressure we need to try and make sure the public understand that the legal profession at large is infinitely more sensitive and responsive than perhaps some of the more prominent dinosaurs make us appear. We do care. We are interested. We do want to see reform, and we're by no means satisfied with the lawyer's traditional image of someone who is only concerned with the administration of the law, and not with the direction it takes. Messages also from Freddy Parker . . . Bill Sopwith . . . a very nice letter here from Jane Smart . . .

(*All through this, the prisoners are slopping out. As the music and crescendo of words threatens to drown everything out,* **Sandra** *suddenly stands up. At once the music stops, and the other areas darken. She straightens her uniform, turns and takes a few paces to the centre of the stage. She stands alone.*)

Sandra:　I want the Chief Superintendent. (*She waits.*) I wonder. Could I have a word? (*Darkness.*)

Text 6

MEASURE FOR MEASURE

[*Enter* **Angelo**, **Mariana**, **Friar Peter**, *and* **Provost**]

Duke:　For this new-married man approaching here,
　　　Whose salt imagination yet hath wronged
　　　Your well-defended honour, you must pardon
　　　For Mariana's sake; but as he adjudged your brother,
　　　Being criminal in double violation
　　　Of sacred chastity and of promise-breach
　　　Thereon dependent, of your brother's life,
　　　The very mercy of the law cries out
　　　Most audible, even from his proper tongue:
　　　'An Angelo for Claudio; death for death.
　　　Haste still pays haste, and leisure answers leisure,
　　　Like doth quit like, and Measure still for Measure.'
　　　Then, Angelo, thy fault's thus manifested,
　　　Which, though thou would'st deny, denies thee vantage.
　　　We do condemn thee to the very block
　　　Where Claudio stooped to death, and with like haste.
　　　Away with him.

Mariana:　O my most gracious lord,
　　　I hope you will not mock me with a husband.

Duke:　It is your husband mocked you with a husband.
　　　Consenting to the safeguard of your honour,
　　　I thought your marriage fit; else imputation,
　　　For that he knew you, might reproach your life,
　　　And choke your good to come. For his possessions,
　　　Although by confiscation they are ours,
　　　We do instate and widow you with all,
　　　To buy you a better husband.

Mariana: O my dear lord, I crave no other, nor no better man.

Duke: Never crave him; we are definitive.

Mariana: Gentle my liege –

Duke: You do but lose your labour.
Away with him to death. [*To Lucio*] Now, sir, to you.

Mariana: [*Kneeling*] O my good lord – sweet Isabel, take my part;
Lend me your knees, and all my life to come
I'll lend you all my life to do you service.

Duke: Against all sense you do importune her.
Should she kneel down in mercy of this fact,
Her brother's ghost his paved bed would break,
And take her hence in horror.

Mariana: Isabel!
Sweet Isabel, do yet but kneel by me;
Hold up your hands, say nothing: I'll speak all.
They say best men are moulded out of faults,
And, for the most, become much more the better
For being a little bad. So may my husband.
O Isabel! Will you not lend a knee?

Duke: He dies for Claudio's death.

Isabella: [*Kneeling*] Most bounteous sir:
Look, if it please you, on this man condemned
As if my brother lived. I partly think
A due sincerity governed his deeds
Till he did look on me. Since it is so,
Let him not die. My brother had but justice,
In that he did the thing for which he died:
For Angelo,
His act did not o'ertake his bad intent,
And must be buried but as an intent
That perished by the way. Thoughts are no subjects;
Intents, but merely thoughts.

Mariana: Merely, my lord.

Duke: Your suit's unprofitable. Stand up, I say.
I have bethought me of another fault.
Provost, how came it Claudio was beheaded
At an unusual hour?

Provost: It was commanded so.

Duke: Had you a special warrant for the deed?

Provost: No, my good lord: it was by private message

Duke: For which I do discharge you of your office.
Give up your keys,

Provost: Pardon me, noble lord;
I thought it was a fault, but knew it not;
Yet did repent me after more advice.
For testimony whereof, one in the prison
That should by private order else have died,

	I have reserved alive.
Duke:	What's he?
Provost:	His name is Barnardine.
Duke:	I would thou hadst done so by Claudio.
	Go, fetch him hither, let me look upon him.

[*Exit* **Provost**]

Escalus:	I am sorry one so learned and so wise
	As you, Lord Angelo, have still appeared,
	Should slip so grossly, both in the heat of blood
	And lack of tempered judgement afterward.
Angelo:	I am sorry that such sorrow I procure,
	And so deep sticks it in my penitent heart
	That I crave death more willingly than mercy;
	'Tis my deserving, and I do entreat it.

[*Enter* **Provost** *with* **Barnardine**, **Claudio**, *muffled, and* **Juliet**]

Duke:	Which is that Barnardine?
Provost:	This, my lord.
Duke:	There was a friar told me of this man.
	Sirrah, thou art said to have a stubborn soul
	That apprehends no further than this world,
	And squar'st thy life according. Thou'rt condemned;
	But, for those earthly faults, I quit them all,
	And pray thee take this mercy to provide
	For better times to come. Friar, advise him;
	I leave him to your hand. – What muffled fellow's that?
Provost:	This is another prisoner that I saved,
	Who should have died when Claudio lost his head;
	As like almost to Claudio as himself. [*Unmuffles* **Claudio**]

Stephen Boxer as Angelo, Cathryn Bradshaw as Mariana and Robert Glenister as the Duke in an RSC production, 1998

Analytical tasks

1   What is going on, do you think, in each of these extracts?

2   Compare the use of vocabulary in each extract. What impact does each writer's lexical choice have on his writing?

3   What other techniques do the writers employ in order to create their effects?

4   Compare and contrast each of these extracts as endings to drama. Consider their impact on the audience as well as linguistic features.

Points of linguistic interest

◆ the use of colloquial English in Text 5; the formality of Text 6
◆ the use of imagery and symbolic language
◆ the syntax
◆ register.

Assignment

Compare and contrast the ways in which Hare and Shakespeare use language to explore issues of gender in *Murmuring Judges* and *Measure for Measure*. In your answer you should consider the contexts of each play and examine and evaluate the ways in which women are presented in both plays.

The next two pieces are poems. 'Havisham' (Text 7) is by Carol Ann Duffy from her collection *Mean Time* and (Text 8) 'Goalkeeper With a Cigarette' is by Simon Armitage from his collection *The Dead Sea Poems*.

Text 7

HAVISHAM

Beloved sweetheart bastard. Not a day since then
I haven't wished him dead. Prayed for it
so hard I've dark green pebbles for eyes,
ropes on the back of my hands I could strangle with.

Spinster. I stink and remember. Whole days
in bed cawing Nooooo at the wall; the dress
yellowing, trembling if I open the wardrobe;
the slewed mirror, full-length, her, myself, who did this

to me? Puce curses that are sounds not words.
Some nights better, the lost body over me,
my fluent tongue in its mouth in its ear
then down till I suddenly bite awake. Love's

hate behind a white veil; a red balloon bursting
in my face. Bang. I stabbed at a wedding-cake.
Give me a male corpse for a long slow honeymoon.
Don't think it's only the heart that b-b-b-breaks.

Text 8

GOALKEEPER WITH A CIGARETTE

That's him in the green,
green cotton jersey,
prince of the clean sheets – some upright insect
boxed between the sticks, the horizontal
and the pitch, stood with something up his sleeve,
armed with a pouch of tobacco and skins
to roll his own, or else a silver tin
containing eight or nine already rolled.
That's him with one behind his ear, between
his lips, or one tucked out of sight and lit –
a stamen cupped in the bud of his fist.
That's him sat down, not like those other clowns,
performing acrobatics on the bar, or press-ups
in the box, or running on the spot,
togged out in turtleneck pyjama-suits
with hands as stunted as a bunch of thumbs,
hands that are bandaged or swaddled with gloves,
laughable, frying-pan, sausage-man gloves.
Not my man, though, that's not what my man does;
a man who stubs his reefers on the post
and kicks his heels in the stud-marks and butts,
lighting the next from the last, in one breath
making the save of the year with his legs,
taking back a deep drag on the goal-line
in the next; on the one hand throwing out
or snaffling the ball from a high corner,
flicking off loose ash with the other. Or
in the freezing cold with both teams snorting
like flogged horses, with captains and coaches
effing and jeffing at backs and forwards,
talking steam, screaming exhausting orders,
that's not breath coming from my bloke, it's smoke.
Not him either goading the terraces,
baring his arse to the visitors' end
and dodging the sharpened ten-pence pieces,
playing up, picking a fight, but that's him
cadging a light from the ambulance men,
loosing off smoke rings, zeros or halos

that drift off, passively, over the goals
into nobody's face, up nobody's nose.
He is what he is, does whatever suits him,
because he has no highfalutin song
to sing, no neat message for the nation
on the theme of genius or dedication;
in his passport, under 'occupation',
no one forced the man to print the word
'custodian', and in *The Faber Book
of Handy Hints* his five-line entry reads:
'You young pretenders, keepers of the nought,
the nish, defenders of the sweet fuck-all,
think bigger than your pockets, profiles, health;
better by half to take a sideways view,
take a tip from me and deface yourselves.'

Analytical tasks

1 What is each poem 'about'?

2 Examine the ways in which Duffy uses language in 'Havisham' to express her ideas.

3 Make a note of any particular phrases that strike you as being effective or noteworthy in any way.

4 Compare the way that Duffy uses language with the way in which Armitage uses it in 'Goalkeeper with a Cigarette'. Comment on specific words and phrases.

Points of linguistic interest

◆ the use of the first person in 'Havisham'
◆ Armitage's use of colloquial language and expletives
◆ the use of half-rhymes
◆ the structure of each poem.

Assignment

Compare and contrast the ways in which Armitage and Duffy create a sense of atmosphere and place in their poetry. In your answer you should refer to their choice of vocabulary, their use of imagery and their use of metaphorical and rhetorical features.

The next two extracts are taken from *Frankenstein* by Mary Shelley (Text 9) and *Dracula* by Bram Stoker (Text 10). In the first, Victor Frankenstein describes his journey through his native mountains, while in the second Harker describes his arrival at Count Dracula's home.

Text 9

FRANKENSTEIN

It was completely dark when I arrived in the environs of Geneva; the gates of the town were already shut, and I was obliged to pass the night at Secheron, a village at the distance of half a league from the city. The sky was serene, and as I was unable to rest, I resolved to visit the spot where my poor William had been murdered. As I could not pass through the town, I was obliged to cross the lake in a boat to arrive at Plainpalais. During this short voyage I saw the lightnings playing on the summit of Mont Blanc in the most beautiful figures. The storm appeared to approach rapidly; and, on landing, I ascended a low hill that I might observe its progress. It advanced; the heavens were clouded, and I soon felt rain coming slowly in large drops, but its violence quickly increased.

I quitted my seat and walked on, although the darkness and storm increased every minute and the thunder burst with a terrific crash over my head. It was echoed from Saleve, the Juras, and the Alps of Savoy; vivid flashes of lightning dazzled my eyes, illuminating the lake, making it appear like a vast sheet of fire; then for an instant every thing seemed of a pitchy darkness, until the eye recovered itself from the preceding flash. The storm, as is often the case in Switzerland, appeared at once in various parts of the heavens. The most violent storm hung exactly north of the town, over that part of the lake which lies between the promontory of Belrive and the village of Copet. Another storm enlightened Jura with faint flashes, and another darkened and sometimes disclosed the Mole, a peaked mountain to the east of the lake.

While I watched the tempest, so beautiful yet terrific, I wandered on with a hasty step. This noble war in the sky elevated my spirits; I clasped my hands and exclaimed aloud, 'William, dear angel! This is thy funeral, this thy dirge.' As I said these words, I perceived in the gloom a figure which stole from behind a clump of trees near me; I stood fixed, gazing intently; I could not be mistaken. A flash of lightning illuminated the object and discovered its shape plainly to me; its gigantic stature, and the deformity of its aspect, more hideous than belongs to humanity, instantly informed me that it was the wretch, the filthy daemon to whom I had given life. What did he there? Could he be (I shuddered at the conception) the murderer of my brother? No sooner did that idea cross my imagination than I became convinced of its truth; my teeth chattered, and I was forced to lean against a tree for support. The figure passed me quickly, and I lost it in the gloom. Nothing in human shape could have destroyed that fair child. He was the murderer I could not doubt it. The mere presence of the idea was an irresistible proof of the fact. I thought of pursuing the devil, but it would have been in vain, for another flash discovered him to me hanging among the rocks of the nearly perpendicular ascent of Mount Saleve, a hill that bound Plainpalais on the south. He soon reached the summit and disappeared.

Text 10

DRACULA

I must have been asleep, for certainly if I had been fully awake I must have noticed the approach to such a remarkable place. In the gloom the courtyard looked of considerable size, and as several dark ways led from it under great round arches it perhaps seemed bigger than it really is. I have not yet been able to see it by daylight.

When the caleche stopped the driver jumped down, and held out his hand to assist me to alight. Again I could not but notice his prodigious strength. His hand actually seemed like a steel vice that could have crushed mine if he had chosen. Then he took out my traps, and placed them on the ground beside me as I stood close to a great door, old and studded with large iron nails, and set in a projecting doorway of massive stone. I could see even in the dim light that the stone was massively carved, but that the carving had been much worn by time and weather. As I stood, the driver jumped again into his seat and shook the reins; the horses started forward, and trap and all disappeared down one of the dark openings.

I stood in silence where I was, for I did not know what to do. Of bell or knocker there was no sign; through these frowning walls and dark window openings it was not likely that my voice could penetrate. The time I waited seemed endless, and I felt doubts and fears crowding upon me. What sort of place had I come to, and among what kind of people? What sort of grim adventure was it on which I had embarked? . . . I began to rub my eyes and pinch myself to see if I were awake. It all seemed like a horrible nightmare to me, and I expected that I should suddenly awake, and find myself at home, with the dawn struggling in through the windows, as I had now and again felt in the morning after a day of overwork. But my flesh answered the pinching test, and my eyes were not to be deceived. I was indeed awake and among the Carpathians. All I could do now was to be patient, and to wait the coming of the morning.

Just as I had come to this conclusion I heard a heavy step approaching behind the great door, and saw through the chinks the gleam of a coming light. Then there was the sound of rattling chains and the clanking of massive bolts drawn back. A key was turned with the loud grating noise of long disuse, and the great door swung back.

Within, stood a tall old man, clean-shaven save for a long white moustache, and clad in black from head to foot, without a single speck of colour about him anywhere. He held in his hand an antique silver lamp, in which the flame burned without chimney or globe of any kind, throwing long, quivering shadows as it flickered in the draught of the open door.

The old man motioned me in with his right hand with a courtly gesture, saying in excellent English, but with a strange intonation:—

'Welcome to my house! Enter freely and of your own will!' He made no motion of stepping to meet me, but stood like a statue, as though his gesture of welcome had fixed him into stone. The instant, however, that I had stepped over the threshold, he moved impulsively forward, and holding out his hand grasped mine with a strength which made me wince, an effect which was not lessened by the fact that it seemed as cold as ice – more like the hand of a dead than a living man. Again he said:–

'Welcome to my house. Come freely. Go safely. And leave something of the happiness you bring!' The strength of the handshake was so much akin to that which I had noticed in the driver, whose face I had not seen, that for a moment I doubted if it were not the same person to whom I was speaking; so, to make sure, I said interrogatively:–

'Count Dracula?' He bowed in a courtly way as he replied:–

'I am Dracula. And I bid you welcome, Mr Harker, to my house. Come in; the night air is chill, and you must need to eat and rest.' As he was speaking he put the lamp on a bracket on the wall, and stepping out, took my luggage; he had carried it in before I could forestall him. I protested, but he insisted:–

'Nay, sir, you are my guest. It is late, and my people are not available. Let me see to your comfort myself.' He insisted on carrying my traps along the passage, and then up a great winding stair, and along another great passage, on whose stone floor our steps rang heavily. At the end of this he threw open a heavy door, and I rejoiced to see within a well-lit room in which a table was spread for supper, and on whose mighty hearth a great fire of logs flamed and flared.

Analytical tasks

1 What effect does the viewpoint from which each of these is written have on the narrative?

2 Examine the atmosphere created in each extract. How does each writer use language in order to create this atmosphere?

3 Comment on any other techniques used by the writers that you have found effective.

4 Write an essay in which you compare and contrast the linguistic techniques that the writers have used to achieve their effects in these extracts.

Points of linguistic interest

◆ the effect of the first person narrative approach
◆ the use of/lack of direct speech
◆ interior monologue approach of Text 9
◆ the use of imagery and symbolism.

Examine the techniques that Shelley employs to give the reader an impression of the creature throughout *Frankenstein* and those used by Stoker to create an impression of Count Dracula throughout *Dracula*. Compare and contrast these techniques, commenting on the similarities and differences between them. Evaluate the effectiveness of each.

The next two extracts are taken from *The Ghost Road* by Pat Barker and *The Railway Man* by Eric Lomax. Each is the closing section of the novel.

Text 11

THE GHOST ROAD

Prior was about to start across the water with ammunition when he was himself hit, though it didn't feel like a bullet, more like a blow from something big and hard, a truncheon or a cricket bat, only it knocked him off his feet and he fell, one arm trailing over the edge of the canal.

He tried to turn to crawl back beyond the drainage ditches, knowing it was only a matter of time before he was hit again, but the gas was thick here and he couldn't reach his mask. Banal, simple, repetitive thoughts ran round and round his mind. *Balls up. Bloody mad. Oh Christ.* There was no pain, more a spreading numbness that left his brain clear. He saw Kirk die. He saw Owen die, his body lifted off the ground by bullets, describing a slow arc in the air as it fell. It seemed to take for ever to fall, and Prior's consciousness fluttered down with it. He gazed at his reflection in the water, which broke and reformed and broke again as bullets hit the surface and then, gradually, as the numbness spread, he ceased to see it.

The light was growing now, the subdued, brownish light of a November dawn. At the far end of the ward, Simpson, too far gone himself to have any understanding of what was happening, jargoned and gobbled away, but all the other faces were turned towards the screens, each man lending the little strength he had to support Hallet in his struggle.

So far, except for the twice repeated whisper and the wordless cries, Hallet had been silent, but now the whisper began again, only more loudly. *Shotvarfet. Shotvarfet.* Again and again, increasing in volume as he directed all his strength into the cry. His mother tried to soothe him, but he didn't hear her. *Shotvarfet. Shotvarfet.* Again and again, each time louder, ringing across the ward. He opened his one eye and gazed directly at Rivers, who had come from behind the screens and was standing at the foot of his bed.

'What's he saying?' Major Hallet asked.

Rivers opened his mouth to say he didn't know and then realized he did. 'He's saying, "It's not worth it." '

'Oh, it is worth it, it *is*,' Major Hallet said, gripping his son's hand. The man was in agony. He hardly knew what he was saying.

'*Shotvarfet.*'

The cry rose again as if he hadn't spoken, and now the other patients were growing restless. A buzz of protest not against the cry, but in support of it, a wordless murmur from damaged brains and drooping mouths.

'*Shotvarfet. Shotvarfet.*'

'I can't stand much more of this,' Major Hallet said. The mother's eyes never left her son's face. Her lips were moving though she made no sound. Rivers was aware of a pressure building in his own throat as that single cry from the patients went on and on. He could not afterwards be sure that he had succeeded in keeping silent, or whether he too had joined in. All he could remember later was gripping the metal rail at the end of the bed till his hands hurt.

And then suddenly it was over. The mangled words faded into silence, and a moment or two later, with an odd movement of the chest and stomach muscles like somebody taking off a too tight jumper, Hallet died.

Rivers reached the bedside before the family realized he was gone, closed the one eye, and from sheer force of habit looked at his watch. '6.25,' he said, addressing Sister Roberts. He raised the sheet as far as Hallet's chin, arranged his arms by his sides and withdrew silently, leaving the family alone with their grief, wishing, as he pulled the screens more closely together, that he had not seen the young girl turn aside to hide her expression of relief.

On the edge of the canal the Manchesters lie, eyes still open, limbs not yet decently arranged, for the stretcher-bearers have departed with the last of the wounded, and the dead are left alone. The battle has withdrawn from them; the bridge they succeeded in building was destroyed by a single shell. Further down the canal another and more successful crossing is being attempted, but the cries and shouts come faintly here.

The sun has risen. The first shaft strikes the water and creeps towards them along the bank, discovering here the back of a hand, there the side of a neck, lending a rosy glow to skin from which the blood has fled, and then, finding nothing here that can respond to it, the shaft of light passes over them and begins to probe the distant fields.

Grey light tinged with rosy pink seeps in through the tall windows. Rivers, slumped at the night nurses' station, struggles to stay awake. On the edge of sleep he hears Njiru's voice, repeating the words of the exorcism of Ave.

O Sumbi! O Cesese! O Palapoko! O Gorepoko! O you Ngengere at the root of the sky. Go down, depart ye.

And there, suddenly, not separate from the ward, not in any way ghostly, not in *fashion blong tomate*, but himself in every particular, advancing down the ward of the Empire Hospital, attended by his shadowy retinue, as Rivers had so often seen him on the coastal path on Eddystone, came Njiru.

There is an end of men, an end of chiefs, an end of chieftains' wives, an end of chiefs' children — then go down and depart. Do not yearn for us, the fingerless, the crippled, the broken. Go down and depart, oh, oh, oh.

He bent over Rivers, staring into his face with those piercing hooded eyes. A long moment, and then the brown face, with its streaks of lime, faded into the light of the daytime ward.

Text 12

THE RAILWAY MAN

In all the time I spent in Japan I never felt a flash of the anger I had harboured against Nagase all those years, no backwash of that surge of murderous intent I had felt on finding out that one of them was still alive. Indeed Nagase gave me the impression of having been prepared for a much more irritated and difficult encounter than ours turned out to be.

Perhaps that is why he seemed afraid, suddenly, when I asked to see him alone in his hotel room in Tokyo, where we were staying prior to our return to Britain. Days before, I had worked out what to do. I had decided to give him a piece of paper which I thought would meet both our needs, and had planned to give it to him in Kyoto; he had wanted very much to show me the great temples of the ancient former capital of Japan.

It rained heavily on the morning of our planned visit to Kyoto, and Nagase felt unwell, so we went with Yoshiko to that extraordinary place. In the rain, the glitter of the Golden Pavilion was softened, its image in the lake blurred. We walked around the stark, simple gardens and looked at everything we could, but I was worried about Nagase's brush with his old cardiac trouble and anxious now to make our final peace.

Looking out the window of our room in the nondescript, modern Tokyo hotel, I could see through a gap created by a building site the coming and going of trains in the huge Tokyo railway station. I sat waiting for Patti and Yoshiko to go out. My request to see Nagase on his own must have carried a charge of electricity, for it disturbed Yoshiko and she said to Patti, with a worried look on her face, 'Heart', and glanced pleadingly at me. I said that it would be all right, but she could not hide her distress.

After they had gone I went next door. There in that quiet room, with the faint noise of trains and the city streets rising up to us, I gave Mr Nagase the forgiveness he desired.

I read my short letter out to him, stopping and checking that he understood each paragraph. I felt he deserved this careful formality. In the letter I said that the war had been over for almost fifty years; that I had suffered much; and that I knew that although he too had suffered throughout this time, he had been most courageous and brave in arguing against militarism and working for reconciliation. I told him that while I could not forget what happened in Kanburi in 1943, I assured him of my total forgiveness.

He was overcome with emotion again, and we spent some time in his room talking quietly and without haste. The next morning we saw Nagase and Yoshiko to their train back to Kurashiki. He phoned us from there that evening to make sure that we were all right. I thought that I had seen him for the last time, perhaps for the last time in our lives. The following day we ourselves made our way to the train for Osaka, from where we would fly to Britain. When after a journey of three hours, the train drew to a halt in Osaka, we stepped on to the platform. At the exact spot where our carriage door opened there was my friend Nagase standing with Yoshiko, smiling and bowing. They knew exactly which coach we were in, and they were like excited children, so pleased to have tricked us; it was good to see them.

They took us to the airport and we left Japan. As the plane tilted us over the bay of Osaka, I held my wife's hand. I felt that I had accomplished more than I could ever have dreamed of. Meeting Nagase has turned him from a hated enemy, with whom friendship would have been unthinkable, into a blood-brother. If I'd never been able to put a name to the face of one of the men who had harmed me, and never discovered that behind that face there was also a damaged life, the nightmares would always have come from a past without meaning. And I had proved for myself that remembering is not enough, if it simply hardens hate.

Back in Thailand, at the Chungkai War Cemetery, when Patti and I walked off on our own, she had had a moment of doubt as she looked at the rows and rows of graves, and wondered whether we were doing the right thing after all. It was only a moment, for we both knew we should be there. I said then: 'Sometime the hating has to stop.'

Analytical tasks

1 What seems to be happening in each passage?

2 How does each writer evoke atmosphere through the descriptive language used?

3 What effects are achieved a) through the use of direct speech, and b) through the narrative viewpoint?

4 Write an essay comparing and contrasting these passages, and evaluate the effectiveness of each as an ending to a novel.

Points of linguistic interest

◆ contrasting narrative viewpoints
◆ use of direct speech/lack of direct speech
◆ focus through single character/range of characters
◆ the use of imagery.

Student response

Here is how one student responded to question 4.

> Text 11 begins in the thick of the action. The character, Prior, seems to be caught up in a battle (I have read the book and know that it is set in the First World War). He is hit at the opening of the passage but Barker, rather than describe the horror of being wounded, describes it rather clinically using the simile of the bullet striking him as feeling like a blow from a cricket bat or truncheons, except that it knocked him off his feet.
>
> →

However, the use of the simile and the other description gives the reader a clear impression, not just of what is going on but what it felt like too.

The description of him crawling back is given an added edge with the almost casual '. . . knowing it was only a matter of time before he was hit again.' The description of Prior's death is a mixture of the factual and the poignant. We are shown his thoughts as he encounters gas but cannot reach for his mask, as he lies there and sees others die and all the time there is the inexorable sense of him drifting into death as numbness spreads throughout his body.

The scene then switches to a hospital where we see another death. We see the soldier, Hallet, rescued from the front fighting for his life in the hospital bed. I'm not clear about the meaning of the whisper 'shotvarfet' but it seems to have some importance here. The man's mother and father seem to be present. The father seems to be a Major (maybe retired). The major holds his son's hand. It is clear that the man is in pain. Again there is the chant of 'shotvarfet'.

Rivers, a doctor, is also present and is part of the pain. Despite all, though, Hallet dies suddenly and without fuss. A simple simile describes his passing – 'The mangled words faded into silence, and a moment or two later with an odd movement of the chest and stomach muscles like somebody taking off a too tight jumper, Hallet died.'

The death is described through Rivers' eyes as he realizes Hallet is dead. There is a ritualized formality in the language describing the arrangement of the sheets, etc. An interesting comment here is the way that he wishes he had not seen '. . . the young girl turn aside to hide her expression of relief.' Presumably this is a reference to Sister Roberts who inwardly felt relief that death had come so peacefully and that this had averted the prospect of a blighted and disabled life.

The scene then switches effectively back to the battlefield where all the dead lie where they have fallen. The futility of these deaths is encapsulated in a single phrase – '. . . the bridge they succeeded in building was destroyed by a single shell.' Colours are important here too as sunrise is described and the sun giving a misleading colour to the flesh of the dead '. . . from which the blood has fled.'

The ending is a little unclear but there seems to be a blending of images within the mind of Rivers, but the final image returns to the daytime and the cold light of day. The third-person narration of this passage allows the writer to give several perspectives of the action and the structure moves from battlefield to hospital and back to battlefield. The final image of the crippled and broken men seen through the mind of Rivers ends the novel on a poignant and reflective note.

→

The extract from 'The Railway Man' is a quite different piece of writing. To begin with it is written in the first person, which means that we see everything through the eyes and mind of Lomax. He begins by explaining that the anger he has felt towards Nagase over many years disappeared when he was in Japan.

He describes his planned meeting with Nagase with whom he had arranged to visit the temples at Kyoto. However, Nagase is unwell on the day of the visit and so Lomax and his wife go with Yoshiko. Throughout his description of this visit he creates a sense of peace and harmony: 'In the rain, the glitter of the Golden Pavilion was softened, its image in the lake blurred.' This reflects Lomax's state of mind here – his feelings of hatred have softened and the edge has gone from his anger. There is a note of tension here too, though, as Lomax, aware of Nagase's heart condition, is anxious to make his final peace with him.

At last Lomax gets his opportunity and there is an element of formality about the forgiveness that he gives to Nagase, emphasized by the reading of a letter. He has obviously written his thoughts down in advance. Lomax here is giving a kind of 'absolution' to his one-time torturer.

Later, on the plane home, it is clear that Lomax has accomplished what he set out to do and his thoughts drift to the war cemetery that he and his wife had visited. He knows that 'Sometimes the hating has to stop.' This seems an effective ending to the novel to me. It concludes Lomax's mission, he has achieved an inner-peace and those closing words have an air of finality about them which signal an end to his suffering. ◆

Examiner's comments

Overall this is a perceptive response which focuses on the question, although coverage of the passages is not even. The student covers Text 11 in some detail and shows a good sense of what is going on, especially the effect of the third-person narration and an awareness of the structure of the piece overall. Some perceptive comments are made on the writer's use of similes, the effects of the language and the atmosphere created. Text 12 is covered in rather less detail, although there is evidence of good understanding and again some perceptive points are made. The response would have been improved by a more even coverage and also a slightly less 'narrative' approach. Nevertheless, there is plenty of evidence of good ideas here.

Examination assignment

Compare and contrast the ways in which Barker and Lomax use language to evoke a sense of the suffering and pain that their characters go through. In your answer you should comment on such features as vocabulary, use of imagery, creation of atmosphere, and narrative viewpoint.

6 Texts and Audience: Dramatic Study

Introduction

The fifth unit of the A Level course (the second unit of A2) is entitled 'Texts and Audience'. The focus of this unit will be the part that considerations of audience play in any piece of writing, and the first part of this unit involves the detailed study of one text from those offered in the syllabus.

In this section of the book you will be given a variety of questions on different texts, using extracts as starting points. In the exam you will not be given extracts, nor will you have access to your text. You will, however, be referred to specific passages or sections. With this proviso, the questions given here are of the kind that you could expect to meet in the exam. If you have not studied the text referred to in a question, use the passage as practice in looking at the different ways writers use language – they are self-contained pieces. If you have studied the text, however, you will find further questions will enable you to practise the kinds of tasks you are likely to face in the exam.

You will need to focus on how writers use the dramatic genre, and to explore such ideas as the ways values are communicated through the play's issues, character interplay and language use. Importance is also placed on the context of the play.

In order to tackle exam questions it is a good idea to have a method of approaching your study of drama. The following outline is one way of tackling the variety of question types that could be asked.

Frameworks

◆ Focus on literary framework and the impact upon audience in terms of drama, character development, exploration of issues, language, etc.

Analysis and explanation

◆ Identify, exemplify and explain the central features of the text, using contextual and structural frameworks
◆ Describe and contextualize these features, e.g. exploration of character, ideas, themes, issues, etc.
◆ Consider meaning and effect
◆ Consider impact upon the audience/theatrical issues.

Evaluation

◆ Evaluate the texts with reference to explanatory frameworks.

The specification offers the following advice:

◆ Candidates will be required to answer on the whole text, analysing theatricality through characters' use of language, presentation of character and development and context of the plot.
◆ Candidates may be required to outline the ways in which issues are raised by dramatists and the attitude they seek to promote as well as the reactions of the audience.

Hints for preparing for the exam

◆ Try to visualize the play; recognize that you are reading something that is essentially designed to be seen and heard rather than read.
◆ Note the impact of the opening scene.
◆ Examine asides and soliloquies.
◆ Look at stage directions.
◆ Look at use of verse and prose.
◆ Examine the lexis of the play.
◆ Examine carefully both the plot and structure of the play.
◆ Think about how the action is presented through language.
◆ Think about the characters – look at key speeches, look for shifts in focus, different ways of interpreting what they do and say.
◆ Look for various possible 'meanings' and 'patterns' in the play.
◆ Consider how or whether the theatrical effects are signalled through the language of the play.
◆ Think about the ways in which the language use affects the pace and variety of action in the play.
◆ Think about relationships between these various elements of the play and how, together, they present a whole.

We will begin by looking at two extracts from *Measure for Measure* by William Shakespeare. Angelo, deputizing for the absent Duke, has condemned Isabella's brother to death and refuses to give a reprieve unless she agrees to sleep with him. In the first extract the Duke, who is disguised as a Friar, consoles Isabella and offers her a way to save her brother. In the second extract, still disguised as a Friar, the Duke speaks to Escalus of the condemned man.

Text 1

MEASURE FOR MEASURE

Duke: Virtue is bold, and goodness never fearful. Have you
not heard speak of Mariana, the sister of Frederick,
the great soldier who miscarried at sea?

Isabella: I have heard of the lady, and good words went with her name.

Duke: She should this Angelo have married: was affianced to her oath, and the nuptial appointed. Between which time of the contract and limit of the solemnity, her brother Frederick was wracked at sea, having in that perished vessel the dowry of his sister. But mark how heavily this befell to the poor gentlewoman. There she lost a noble and renowned brother, in his love toward her ever most kind and natural; with him, the portion and sinew of her fortune, her marriage dowry; with both, her combinate husband, this well-seeming Angelo.

Isabella: Can this be so? Did Angelo so leave her?

Duke: Left her in her tears, and dried not one of them with his comfort: swallowed his vows whole, pretending in her discoveries of dishonour; in few, bestowed her on her own lamentation, which she yet wears for his sake; and he, a marble to her tears, is washed with them, but relents not.

Isabella: What a merit were it in death to take this poor maid from the world! What corruption in this life, that it will let this man live! But how out of this can she avail?

Duke: It is a rupture that you may easily heal: and the cure of it not only saves your brother, but keeps you from dishonour in doing it.

Isabella: Show me how, good father.

Duke: This forenamed maid hath yet in her the continuance of her first affection. His unjust unkindness, that in all reason should have quenched her love, hath, like an impediment in the current, made it more violent and unruly. Go you to Angelo; answer his requiring with a plausible obedience; agree with his demands to the point. Only refer yourself to this advantage: first, that your stay with him may not be long; that the place may have all shadow and silence in it; and the time answer to convenience. This being granted in course, and now follows all. We shall advise this wronged maid to stead up your appointment, go in your place. If the encounter acknowledge itself hereafter, it may compel him to her recompense; and hear, by this is your brother saved, your honour untainted, the poor Mariana advantaged, and the corrupt deputy scaled. The maid will I frame, and make fit for his attempt. If you think well to

carry this as you may, the doubleness of the benefit
defends the deceit from reproof.

Text 2

MEASURE FOR MEASURE

Duke: He professes to have received no sinister measure
           from his judge, but most willingly humbles himself
           to the determination of justice. Yet had he
           framed to himself, by the instruction of his frailty,
           many deceiving promises of life, which I, by my
           good leisure, have discredited to him; and now is
           he resolved to die.

Escalus: You have paid the heavens your function, and
           the prisoner the very debt of your calling. I have
           laboured for the poor gentleman to the
           extremest shore of my modesty, but my brother-
           justice have I found so severe that he hath forced
           me to tell him he is indeed Justice.

Duke: If his own life answer the straitness of his
           proceeding, it shall become him well; wherein if
           he chance to fail, he hath sentenced himself.

Escalus: I am going to visit the prisoner; fare you well.

Duke: Peace be with you. [*Exit **Escalus***]
           He who the sword of heaven will bear
           Should be as holy as severe:
           Pattern in himself to know,
           Grace to stand, and virtue, go:
           More nor less to others paying
           Than by self-offences weighing.
           Shame to him whose cruel striking
           Kills for faults of his own liking!
           Twice treble shame on Angelo,
           To weed my vice, and let his grow!
           O, what may man within him hide,
           Though angel on the outward side!
           How may likeness made in crimes
           Making practice on the times
           To draw with idle spiders' strings
           Most ponderous and substantial things?
           Craft against vice I must apply.
           With Angelo tonight shall lie
           His old betrothed, but despised:
           So disguise shall, by th'disguised,
           Pay with falsehood false exacting,
           And perform an old contracting.

Analytical tasks

1 What is being said in both these extracts?

2 What view of justice does the Duke express in both extracts?

3 What is the function of the Duke's soliloquy at the end of Text 2?

4 Write a short essay examining the language that the Duke uses in these two extracts, and commenting on the effect that it would have on the audience.

Points of linguistic interest

◆ the directness and clarity of the Duke's language
◆ his use of imagery
◆ the formality/informality of his register
◆ the use of the soliloquy.

Assignment

Examine the ways in which Shakespeare uses language to allow the audience to build up a picture of the Duke throughout the play. You should refer to such features as form, style and vocabulary in your answer.

The next two extracts are taken from *The Revenger's Tragedy* by Tourneur. Vindice, the central character, is speaking in each of them.

Text 3

THE REVENGER'S TRAGEDY

Vindice: Does every proud and self-affecting dame
Camphor her face for this, and grieve her maker
In sinful baths of milk, when many an infant starves
For her superfluous outside – all for this?
Who now bids twenty pound a night, prepares
Music, perfumes and sweetmeats? All are hushed,
Thou may'st lie chaste now! It were fine methinks
To have thee seen at revels, forgetful feasts
And unclean brothels; sure 'twould fright the sinner
And make him a good coward, put a reveller
Out of his antic amble
And cloy an epicure with empty dishes.
Here might a scornful and ambitious woman
Look through and through herself; see, ladies, with false forms
You deceive men but cannot deceive worms.

Now to my tragic business. Look you brother,
I have not fashioned this only for show
And useless property, no – it shall bear a part
E'en in it own revenge. This very skull,
Whose mistress the duke poisoned with this drug,
The mortal curse of the earth, shall be revenged
In the like strain and kiss his lips to death.
As much as the dumb thing can, he shall feel;
What fails in poison we'll supply in steel.

Text 4

THE REVENGER'S TRAGEDY

Vindice: May not we set as well as the duke's son?
Thou hast no conscience: are we not revenged?
Is there one enemy left alive amongst those?
'Tis time to die when we are ourselves our foes.
When murderers shut deeds close this curse does seal 'em:
If none disclose 'em, they themselves reveal 'em!
This murder might have slept in tongueless brass
But for ourselves, and the world died an ass.
Now I remember too, here was Plato
Brought forth a knavish sentence once:
No doubt – said he – but time
Will make the murderer bring forth himself.
'Tis well he died, he was a witch!
And now my lord, since we are in for ever
This work was ours, which else might have been slipped;
And if we list we could have nobles clipped
And go for less than beggars.

Analytical tasks

1 What is Vindice saying in each of these speeches?

2 What aspects of his character are revealed?

3 Comment on his use of language in each speech. What kinds of differences are there between Text 3 and Text 4?

4 Write a short piece examining the effects of the language use in each of these extracts.

Points of linguistic interest

◆ the effect of the choice of vocabulary
◆ the effects created by the form and rhyme

◆ the use of imagery
◆ the tone created by each extract.

The following extract is taken from *The Recruiting Officer* by George Farquhar. Here we see Captain Plume, a recruiting officer, discussing women with Mr Worthy, a gentleman.

Text 5

THE RECRUITING OFFICER

Worthy: Thou art a happy fellow; once I was so.

Plume: What ails thee, man? No inundations nor earthquakes in Wales, I hope? Has your father rose from the dead, and reassumed his estate?

Worthy: No.

Plume: Then you are married, surely.

Worthy: No.

Plume: Then you are mad, or turning Quaker.

Worthy: Come, I must out with it – your once gay, roving friend is dwindled into an obsequious, thoughtful, romantic, constant coxcomb.

Plume: And pray, what is all this for?

Worthy: For a woman.

Plume: Shake hands, brother, if you go to that – behold me as obsequious, as thoughtful, and as constant a coxcomb as your worship.

Worthy: For whom?

Plume: For a regiment. But for a woman! 'Sdeath! I have been constant to fifteen at a time, but never melancholy for one; and can the love of one bring you into this pickle? Pray, who is this miraculous Helen?

Worthy: A Helen indeed, not to be won under a ten years' siege; as great a beauty, and as great a jilt.

Plume: A jilt! Pho! Is she as great a whore?

Worthy: No, no.

Plume: 'Tis ten thousand pities; but who is she? Do I know her?

Worthy: Very well.

Plume: Impossible! – I know no woman that will hold out a ten years' siege.

Worthy: What think you of Melinda?

Plume: Melinda! Why, she began to capitulate this time twelvemonth, and offered to surrender upon honourable terms; and I advised you to propose a settlement of five hundred pound a year to her, before I went last abroad.

Worthy: I did, and she hearkened to't, desiring only one week to consider; when beyond her hopes the town was relieved, and I forced to turn my siege into a blockade.

Plume: Explain, explain.

Worthy: My Lady Richly, her aunt in Flintshire, dies, and leaves her at this critical time twenty thousand pound.

Plume: Oh, the devil! What a delicate woman was there spoiled! But by the rules of war now, Worthy, blockade was foolish – after such a convoy of provisions was entered the place, you could have no thought of reducing it by famine – you should have redoubled your attacks, taken the town by storm, or have died upon the breach.

Worthy: I did make one general assault, and pushed it with all my forces; but I was so vigorously repulsed, that despairing of ever gaining her for a mistress, I have altered my conduct, given my addresses the obsequious and distant turn, and court her now for a wife.

Plume: So, as you grew obsequious, she grew haughty, and because you approached her as a goddess, she used you like a dog.

Worthy: Exactly.

Plume: 'Tis the way of 'em all. Come, Worthy, your obsequious and distant airs will never bring you together; you must not think to surmount her pride by your humility. Would you bring her to better thoughts of you, she must be reduced to a meaner opinion of herself – let me see – the very first thing that I would do, should be to lie with her chambermaid, and hire three or four wenches in the neighbourhood to report that I had got them with child. Suppose we lampooned all the pretty women in town, and left her out? Or what if we made a ball, and forgot to invite her, with one or two of the ugliest?

Worthy: These would be mortifications, I must confess; but we live in such a precise, dull place that we can have no balls, no lampoons, no –

Plume: What! No bastards! And so many recruiting officers in town; I thought 'twas a maxim among them to leave as many recruits in the country as they carried out.

Worthy: Nobody doubts your goodwill, noble Captain, in serving your country with your best blood: witness our friend Molly at the Castle, there have been tears in town about that business, Captain.

Plume: I hope Silvia has not heard of it.

Worthy: Oh sir, have you thought of her? I began to fancy you had forgot poor Silvia.

Analytical tasks

1 What is being said in this extract?

2 How do Plume's and Worthy's attitudes towards women differ?

3 Examine the ways in which language is used here. What comments have you to make about it?

4 Pick out any words or phrases that you find particularly effective.

Points of linguistic interest

◆ the use of imagery
◆ the comic phrasing
◆ the use of inflated language
◆ the language of the soldier and the language of the gentleman.

Assignment

Explore the ways in which Farquhar uses language in order to differentiate between characters in the play. You can focus on two or three characters, or you can range more widely if you wish. In your answer you should consider how choice of vocabulary and style help to shape the meaning of the text.

The next two extracts are from *Othello*. In the first (Text 6), which is the opening of the play, we see Iago talking to Roderigo about Othello. In the next (Text 7), a soliloquy, Iago expresses further views about Othello as he begins his plot against him.

Text 6

OTHELLO

[*Enter **Roderigo** and **Iago**]*

Roderigo: Tush, never tell me! I take it much unkindly
That thou, Iago, who hast had my purse
As if the strings were thine, shouldst know of this.

Iago: 'Sblood, but you will not hear me!
If ever I did dream of such a matter,
Abhor me.

Roderigo: Thou told'st me thou didst hold him in thy hate.

Iago: Despise me, if I do not. Three great ones of the city,
In personal suit to make me his Lieutenant,
Off-capped to him; and by the faith of man,
I know my price, I am worth no worse a place.
But he, as loving his own pride and purposes,
Evades them with a bombast circumstance
Horribly stuffed with epithets of war,
Non-suits my mediators. For 'Certes,' says he,
'I have already chose my officer.'
And what was he?
Forsooth, a great arithmetician,
One Michael Cassio, a Florentine –
A fellow almost damned in a fair wife –
That never set a squadron in the field,
Nor the division of a battle knows

	More than a spinster – unless the bookish theoric,
	Wherein the toged consuls can propose
	As masterly as he. Mere prattle without practice
	Is all his soldiership. But he, sir, had th'election:
	And I, of whom his eyes had seen the proof
	At Rhodes, at Cyprus, and on other grounds
	Christian and heathen, must be leed and calmed
	By debitor and creditor; this counter-caster,
	He in good time must his Lieutenant be,
	And I – God bless the mark! – his Moorship's Ancient.
Roderigo:	By heaven, I rather would have been his hangman.
Iago:	Why, there's no remedy. 'Tis the curse of service;
	Preferment goes by letter and affection,
	And not by old gradation, where each second
	Stood heir to th'first. Now sir, be judge yourself
	Whether I in any just term am affined
	To love the Moor.
Roderigo:	I would not follow him then.
Iago:	O, sir, content you:
	I follow him to serve my turn upon him.
	We cannot all be masters, nor all masters
	Cannot be truly followed. You shall mark
	Many a duteous and knee-crooking knave
	That, doting on his own obsequious bondage,
	Wears out his time, much like his master's ass,
	For naught but provender, and when he's old – cashiered!
	Whip me such honest knaves. Others there are
	Who, trimmed in forms and visages of duty,
	Keep yet their hearts attending on themselves,
	And, throwing but shows of service on their lords,
	Do well thrive by them; and when they have lined their coats,
	Do themselves homage: these fellows have some soul,
	And such a one do I profess myself.
	For sir
	It is as sure as you are Roderigo,
	Were I the Moor, I would not be Iago:
	In following him, I follow but myself.
	Heaven is my judge, not I for love and duty,
	But seeming so for my peculiar end:
	For when my outward action doth demonstrate
	The native act and figure of my heart
	In compliment extern, 'tis not long after,
	But I will wear my heart upon my sleeve
	For daws to peck at – I am not what I am.

Richard McCabe as Iago with Aidan McArdle as Roderigo, RSC at the Barbican, 2000

Text 7

OTHELLO

Iago: Thus do I ever make my fool my purse:
         For I mine own gained knowledge should profane
         If I would time expend with such a snipe
         But for my sport and profit. I hate the Moor,
         And it is thought abroad that 'twixt my sheets
         He's done my office. I know not if't be true
         But I, for mere suspicion in that kind,
         Will do as if for surety. He holds me well:
         The better shall my purpose work on him.
         Cassio's a proper man: let me see now;
         To get his place and to plume up my will
         In double knavery. How? How? Let's see.
         After some time, to abuse Othello's ear
         That he is too familiar with his wife;
         He hath a person and a smooth dispose
         To be suspected, framed to make women false.
         The Moor is of a free and open nature,
         That thinks men honest that but seem to be so,
         And will as tenderly be led by th'nose
         As asses are.
         I have't. It is engendered. Hell and night
         Must bring this monstrous birth to the world's light. [*Exit*]

Analytical tasks

1   Make a list of all the grievances that Iago claims to have against Othello, as mentioned in both extracts.

2   What do you find surprising about Iago's response to the rumour that Othello has slept with Iago's wife?

> **3** Examine the language that Iago uses when talking about a) Othello and b) Michael Cassio.
>
> **4** What kind of character does Iago appear to be, based on the evidence of these two extracts? Use specific examples from the extracts to support your ideas.

Points of linguistic interest

◆ Iago's use of military (and other) imagery
◆ the language he uses to refer to Othello
◆ the structure and verse form used
◆ the vocabulary.

Student response

Here is one student's response to the questions above.

Question 1

Text 6

◆ Three influential men in the city had canvassed Othello to make Iago his Deputy, but to no avail.
◆ Iago feels he is well worth the position of Lieutenant.
◆ Othello is full of his own importance.
◆ He has already given the job to Michael Cassio.
◆ Iago feels that although Cassio might be well-versed in the theory of war, he has no practical experience as a soldier – unlike Iago himself.

Text 7

◆ It is rumoured that Othello has slept with Iago's wife.
◆ He recognizes the Othello is honest and sees good in all men and therefore can be '. . . tenderly led by the nose/As asses are'.

Question 2

Iago doesn't seem particularly bothered that it is rumoured that Othello has slept with his wife. He says he does not know whether it is true or not but it is sufficient for him just to suspect Othello of being guilty. You would think he would want to know for sure whether it were true or not, but he seems to mention it almost in passing. It is as if he is just thankful to have another excuse to hate Othello.

Question 3

a) He is quite derogatory about Othello and makes it seem as if he does not listen to anyone. For example, the three dignitaries who went to recommend Iago for the position of Lieutenant were ignored. He also says

→

---

that Othello evaded them with '. . . bombast circumstance/Horribly stuffed with epithets of war.' This gives the impression of Othello as a bombastic person who listens to nothing but the sound of his own voice. It is also noticeable that Iago always refers to Othello as the Moor, rather than as Othello. This serves to constantly draw attention to the fact that he is, in some respects, an alien, and outsider, he is not 'one of them', i.e. a Venetian.

b) He speaks of Cassio in uncomplimentary terms too. He calls him a 'Florentine' which seems to be some kind of criticism – maybe because he is not a native of Venice. Another unusual insult is where he calls him an 'arithmetician', meaning that he knows about the theoretical concepts of war but has not had the practical experience that would make him a good choice as Lieutenant. He says that he knows no more about how to divide forces up in battle than 'a spinster.'

Question 4

On the evidence of these two extracts Iago seems to be a vindictive sort of person who reacts badly to not getting his own way. He certainly holds it against Othello that he was not promoted to Lieutenant. More dangerously, though, he is the kind of character who does not let his feelings be known but instead schemes for revenge behind people's backs. He freely admits that he is not as he seems to be when he says 'I am not what I am.' The ease with which he is prepared to believe the rumours about Othello and his wife, and the relish with which he seems to begin to plot revenge, seem to suggest that he actually, in a perverse kind of way, enjoys the scheming. From these accounts he also holds himself in high regard when it comes to possessing the skills of a soldier. ◆

Examiner's comments

Overall the student tackles these questions well although some of them could have been answered in a little more detail.

In Question 1 the student covers the key points and has recognized the main areas of grievance. The student's response to Question 2 shows a good level of perception, and she picks up some subtle points here – clearly aware of the innuendo behind Iago's words. There is good focus on language shown in Question 3. Again the student makes a number of important points and supports them with reference to the language of the play. Her assessment of Iago's character is sound, and based closely on what can be seen from these extracts. Good perception is shown throughout.

Assignment

Examine the ways in which Othello's language changes throughout the play and how this reflects his changing state of mind. You should refer to vocabulary, imagery, syntax and form in your answer.

The next extract is taken from *As You Like It* by William Shakespeare. Here we see Celia trying to cheer up her cousin, Rosalind, who is feeling unhappy because of the banishment of her father.

Text 8

AS YOU LIKE IT

*[Enter **Rosalind** and **Celia**]*

Celia:	I pray thee, Rosalind, sweet my coz, be merry.
Rosalind:	Dear Celia, I show more mirth than I am mistress of, and would you yet I were merrier? Unless you could teach me to forget a banished father, you must not learn me how to remember any extraordinary pleasure.
Celia:	Herein I see thou lovest me not with the full weight that I love thee. If my uncle, thy banished father, had banished thy uncle, the Duke my father, so thou hadst been still with me, I could have taught my love to take thy father for mine; so wouldst thou, if the truth of thy love to me were so righteously tempered as mine is to thee.
Rosalind:	Well, I will forget the condition of my estate, to rejoice in yours.
Celia:	You know my father hath no child but I, nor none is like to have; and truly, when he dies, thou shalt be his heir: for what he hath taken away from thy father perforce, I will render thee again in affection, by mine honour I will, and when I break that oath, let me turn monster. Therefore, my sweet Rose, my dear Rose, be merry.
Rosalind:	From henceforth I will, coz, and devise sports. Let me see – what think you of falling in love ?
Celia:	Marry, I prithee do, to make sport withal; but love no man in good earnest, nor no further in sport neither, than with safety of a pure blush thou mayst in honour come off again.
Rosalind:	What shall be our sport then ?
Celia:	Let us sit and mock the good housewife Fortune from her wheel, that her gifts may henceforth be bestowed equally.
Rosalind:	I would we could do so; for her benefits are mightily misplaced, and the bountiful blind woman doth most mistake in her gifts to women.
Celia:	'Tis true, for those that she makes fair she scarce makes honest, and those that she makes honest she makes very ill-favouredly.
Rosalind:	Nay, now thou goest from Fortune's office to Nature's: Fortune reigns in gifts of the world, not in the lineaments of Nature.

[*Enter **Touchstone***]

Celia:	No; when Nature hath made a fair creature, may she not by Fortune fall into the fire? Though Nature hath given us wit to flout at Fortune, hath not Fortune sent in this fool to cut off the argument?
Rosalind:	Indeed, there is Fortune too hard for Nature, when Fortune makes Nature's natural the cutter-off of Nature's wit.
Celia:	Peradventure this is not Fortune's work neither, but Nature's, who perceiveth our natural wits too dull to reason of such goddesses and hath sent this natural for our whetstone; for always the dullness of the fool is the whetstone of the wits. How now, wit, whither wander you ?
Touchstone:	Mistress, you must come away to your father.
Celia:	Were you made the messenger?
Touchstone:	No, by mine honour, but I was bid to come for you.
Rosalind:	Where learned you that oath, fool?
Touchstone:	Of a certain knight that swore by his honour they were good pancakes and swore by his honour the mustard was naught; now I'll stand to it the pancakes were naught and the mustard was good, and yet was not the knight forsworn.
Celia:	How prove you that, in the great heap of your knowledge ?
Rosalind:	Ay, marry, now unmuzzle your wisdom.
Touchstone:	Stand you both forth now: stroke your chins and swear by your beards that I am a knave.
Celia:	By our beards – if we had them – thou art.
Touchstone:	By my knavery – if I had it – then I were; but if you swear by that that is not, you are not forsworn; no more was this knight, swearing by his honour, for he never had any; or if he had, he had sworn it away before ever he saw those pancakes or that mustard.
Celia:	Prithee, who is't that thou meanest?
Touchstone:	One that old Frederick, your father, loves.
Celia:	My father's love is enough to honour him enough. Speak no more of him; you'll be whipped for taxation one of these days.
Touchstone:	The more pity that fools may not speak wisely what wise men do foolishly.
Celia:	By my troth, thou sayest true: for since the little wit that fools have was silenced, the little foolery that wise men have makes a great show.

Analytical tasks

1 What is being said, in general terms, in this extract?

2 Pick out three puns that are used here and explain the effect of each of them.

> **3** Can you detect a difference between Rosalind and Celia from their use of language here?
>
> **4** What does Touchstone add to the extract?

Points of linguistic interest

◆ the punning and the wordplay
◆ the verbal fencing between the two girls
◆ their attitudes towards love
◆ the arrival of Touchstone.

Assignment

Examine the attitudes towards love put forward through both the language and theatrical effect of *As You Like It*. In your answer you should refer to form, style and vocabulary.

This next extract is from *The Alchemist* by Ben Jonson. Here, Subtle and Surly discuss the art of the alchemist.

Text 9

THE ALCHEMIST

Subtle:	Why, what have you observed, sir, in our art, seems so impossible?
Surly:	But your whole work, no more.
	That you should hatch gold in a furnace, sir,
	As they do eggs, in Egypt!
Subtle:	Sir, do you
	Believe that eggs are hatch'd so?
Surly:	If I should?
Subtle:	Why, I think that the greater miracle.
	No egg but differs from a chicken more
	Than metals in themselves.
Surly:	That cannot be.
	The egg's ordain'd by nature, to that end:
	And is a chicken *in potentia*.
Subtle:	The same we say of lead, and other metals,
	Which would be gold, if they had time.
Mammon:	And that
	Our art doth further.
Subtle:	Ay, for 'twere absurd
	To think that nature, in the earth, bred gold
	Perfect, i' the instant. Something went before.
	There must be remote matter.

Surly:	Ay, what is that?
Subtle:	Marry, we say –
Mammon:	Ay, now it heats: stand, Father.

Pound him to dust –

Subtle:	It is, of the one part,

A humid exhalation, which we call
Materia liquida, or the unctuous water;
On th' other part, a certain crass and viscous
Portion of earth; both which, concorporate,
Do make the elementary matter of gold:
Which is not, yet, *propria materia*,
But commune to all metals, and all stones.
For, where it is forsaken of that moisture,
And hath more dryness, it becomes a stone;
Where it retains more of the humid fatness,
It turns to sulphur, or to quick-silver:
Who are the parents of all other metals.
Nor can this remote matter, suddenly,
Progress so from extreme, unto extreme,
As to grow gold, and leap o'er all the means.
Nature doth, first, beget th' imperfect; then
Proceeds she to the perfect. Of that airy
And oily water, mercury is engend'red:
Sulphur o' the fat, and earthy part: the one
(Which is the last) supplying the place of male,
The other of the female, in all metals.
Some do believe hermaphrodeity,
That both do act, and suffer. But, these two
Make the rest ductile, malleable, extensive.
And, even in gold, they are; for we do find
Seeds of them, by our fire, and gold in them:
And can produce the species of each metal
More perfect thence, than nature doth in earth.
Beside, who doth not see, in daily practice,
Art can beget bees, hornets, beetles, wasps,
Out of the carcasses and dung of creatures:
Yea, scorpions of an herb, being rightly plac'd?
And these are living creatures, far more perfect
And excellent than metals.

Mammon:	Well said, Father!

Nay, if he take you in hand, sir, with an argument,
He'll bray you in a mortar.

Surly:	Pray you, sir, stay.

Rather, than I'll be bray'd, sir, I'll believe,
That alchemy is a pretty kind of game,
Somewhat like tricks o' the cards, to cheat a man
With charming.

Subtle:	Sir?
Surly:	What else are all your terms,
	Whereon no one o' your writers 'grees with other?
	Of your elixir, your *lac virginis*,
	Your stone, your med'cine, and your chrysosperm,
	Your sal, your sulphur, and your mercury,
	Your oil of height, your tree of life, your blood,
	Your marchesite, your tutie, your magnesia,
	Your toad, your crow, your dragon, and your panther,
	Your sun, your moon, your firmament, your adrop,
	Your *lalo, azoch, zemich, chibrit, heautarit*,
	And then your red man, and your white woman,
	With all your broths, your menstrues, and materials,
	Of piss, and egg-shells, women's terms, man's blood,
	Hair o' the head, burnt clouts, chalk, merds, and clay,
	Poulder of bones, scalings of iron, glass,
	And worlds of other strange ingredients,
	Would burst a man to name?
Subtle:	And all these, nam'd,
	Intending but one thing: which art our writers
	Us'd to obscure their art.

Analytical tasks

1   What is being said in this exchange?

2   What do you notice about the kind of language that Subtle uses?

3   What do you think the intended effect is, both on the other characters and the audience? Is it successful?

4   There are probably many words and phrases here that you do not understand. It is unlikely that many audiences of Jonson's time would have understood them either. Does it matter?

Points of linguistic interest

◆ the 'technical' alchemist language
◆ the elevated tone
◆ the verse form
◆ the imagery.

Examination assignment

How does Jonson use language to convey a sense of mood and purpose in *The Alchemist*? In your answer you should refer to vocabulary, form and style as well as any other features you feel are important.

7 Adaptation of Texts for an Audience

Introduction

This part of the examination comes as the second section to Unit 5, which has as its foundation the study of the ways in which texts address themselves to their audience. You can count on the fact that there will be some clear relationship between the original texts and the new text that you are asked to produce, and the new text is likely to have a new purpose and audience.

The skills you need to practise, therefore, are those of selecting material from the given texts, choosing an appropriate new address towards your new audience, and the production of a new text. In the exam, you will have a great deal to do in a short period of time, so it is vital that you acquaint yourself with all the different types of text (see Chapter 1) and that you feel confident about writing for new audiences, as well as adapting your register for a new purpose. You will always be asked to reflect on your new text by comparing it to parts of the source texts. It is therefore doubly important that you make your text sufficiently different from the original. The question will give you many hints as to the nature of the changes required.

The following texts will provide the practice that you require for this section of the paper. If you can also carry out some textual analysis of each text, this will give you added confidence and of course improve your analytical skills for the synoptic unit.

Assignment

◆ Read the following two texts – they are both about names. You have been asked to write a short article on names, and our feelings towards names, for a textbook aimed at Year 6 pupils (the last year of primary school, children aged 10–11 years). You are required to make your article as informative as possible. You should aim to write about 400 words, but this is only a rough guideline.

◆ Using both of the original texts, compare the ways you have chosen to present your information with that given in the original articles. You should focus on three or four carefully chosen examples from your own text to illustrate your points.

Text 1

CHANGING NAMES

Question: what has Prince Charles got in common with a rock singer, a heavyweight boxer and young William Pooter in *Diary of a Nobody*? Answer: the desire to change his name; in his case, to Windsor-Mountbatten. In Cassius Clay's to Muhammad Ali; Cat Stevens became Yusaf Islam and little William Pooter declared henceforth to be known as Lupin.

People can have a terrible time with the names their parents give them. Poor John Smith – and all John Smiths; at least you could say, as John Wyndham said of girls named Petunia, that anyone of that name who got anywhere must have something her parents didn't have. When a child is given a beautiful, unusual old name, the parents may think it's unique – only to find half a dozen other Lucys, Jasons and Emmas in the class. And any parent that saddles a child with a name that will need explaining for the rest of its life has a lot to answer for. It's a bit steep to call your child after your heroes – Karl Marx Miller, for example.

Subtler sufferings are felt by those whose names are simply, they feel, not them. There's a theory that the names parents give children mirror their expectations of them: in *Women and Words*, Miller and Swift suggest a Jody is expected to be confident and outgoing, a Letitia feminine and dependent. Really? But one parent may have known a shy, fluttering Jody, while another remembers a Letitia who played hockey for Lancashire and ran an iron foundry.

Like it or not, we do attach connotations to names. And a good many of our instinctive reactions are a lot more class-ridden than we realise: 'Sid' for yer average yobbo too dumb to understand about buying gas shares and 'Tracey' epitomising Essex girl.

Text 2

WHAT'S IN A NAME?

A name is a very personal thing and people don't normally *name* a place they don't like. There can't be many high-rise flats, for example, where anyone living on the top floors has removed the flat number and firmly stuck on a name plate saying 'Seagull's Nest'.

Terraced houses aren't usually personalised either. The most famous house in England, for example, has no name. It's 10 Downing Street. Turn away from the urban streets, where 89 High Street is better known for the fine display of geraniums in the first floor window box than by its number (which has fallen off anyway), and you're in the territory of *Windy Ridge* and *Woodbine Cottage*, a land of hillside and laurels, orchards and yew trees, which offers its inhabitants both vicarage and school house, sunny side and fair view.

We know this because the Halifax Building Society did a computer run of 15.5

million of its recent and current investors and borrowers to find out what they call their homes. The Halifax found strong evidence that home is the last place people want to link with their working life. If home is where the heart is, then the heart wants to rest in peace with its lawn-mower in *Stone Haven* or *The Anchorage* where they have *Dunroamin* and have settled *Chez Nous*.

Nowhere in the Society's top 100 was there a name such as *Concorde Flight Path* or *Micro Roost*, to reflect the 20th Century: there were no *Railway Views* or *Workers' Cottages*, which might have reflected the 19th Century (although the Industrial Revolution did leave an echo in names like *Mill House*). The top five names nationally are: *The Bungalow*, *The Cottage*, *Rose Cottage*, *The School House*, and *The White House*.

Religious connections are prominent elsewhere: for example, *The Old Rectory* and *The Old Vicarage*. Other names which no self-respecting list of house names would be without are *Primrose Cottage*, *Sea View* and *Casa Mia*. Many others have a name derived from trees, including *The Larches*, *Woodlands*, *Tree Tops*, *The Orchard*, *Cherry Trees*, *Oak Wood* and *Beech Croft*. There may be no more orchards in the street than there are shepherds in Shepherds Bush or crops in London's Cornhill waving amongst the finance houses, but it all helps to remind us that we have roots, whoever we are, in the place where we live.

Assignment

◆ *The English Review*, a magazine written for Advanced Level English students by eminent academics, has set up a competition for Advanced Level English students to write about 'The changing nature of the English language'. You have been given the following two articles as your sources for your own piece of writing. The audience you are writing for is fairly academic but of your own age; you are free to take whatever line you wish as long as it addresses the given title.

◆ In an analysis of your own writing, focus on some of the ways you have chosen to ensure your material is suited to its audience.

Text 3

TEEN TALK'S ALL GREEK TO ADULTS

So you think you're sorted when it comes to keeping up with the teenagers of today?

When they talk about larging it up in a chill-out room or say they are mad for it, you're not left scratching your head.

Well shave off! Roll a fat one! You may think you're still with it but you have a real whitee – you are nowhere near as moshin' as they are.

For those who don't understand just ask your children – these phrases are becoming common currency in the playground.

A new study has discovered a bewildering array of words which are being invented and passed on.

Researchers have found that the use of the internet and other new media by children means that our language is changing more rapidly than ever before.

Richard Hogg, professor of English at Manchester, said: 'It's no surprise parents have difficulty. The astonishing rise of new media means today's teenagers are exposed to many influences from around the world and are absorbing more of it than ever before.'

Professor Hogg says children and teenagers have always looked for new words, especially to describe feelings of elation or angst.

'Children add new words to their vocabulary to stay one step ahead and distinguish themselves from parents and the establishment.'

The Survey of Britain's teenagers was conducted by drinks manufacturer Vimto for an ad campaign.

Spokesman Andy Hoe said: 'Parents themselves will start using words they overhear their children using once they understand them. If these words are used often enough and stand the test of time, then they will become an accepted part of everyday language.'

SIMPLY MOSHIN'!

The Vimto Survey found new words currently all the rage with teenagers include:

Bow Down meaning *great*, as in 'That was a bow down concert.'
Moshin' meaning *cool!* as in 'Those clothes are moshin'.'
Steam Up is *really exciting* as in 'That Party was a real steam up.'
Uber babe – good-looking girl as in 'She's an uber babe.'
Bitchin – really good as in 'That's a bitchin' CD.'
Really on! – trendy as in 'That club is really on.'
Roll a fat one – Play another record.
Whitee – a problem as in 'I'm having a whitee.'

Text 4

GOBSMACKED BY SHRIMPING DWEEBS

New words that have come into use in the Nineties indicate that, these days, it is not what you are that counts but how you behave. Words describing people as if they were things – yuppie, dinky – went out with the Eighties. Non-aspirational Nineties people care less how others categorise them – but are likely to get 'in your face' if thwarted, say, from 'cocooning' in order to stave off 'compassion fatigue' and recover a little 'feelgood'.

A new dictionary with 200,000 references published this month, *Chambers' Encyclopedic English Dictionary (£25)*, contains 'squeegies' (crossroads windscreen cleaners – unemployed yuppies?) as a rare remnant of Eighties-style typecasting, and 'shrimping', a Nineties behaviour word unusual for being frivolous amid the dour Nineties expressions for caring and sharing. Shrimping, says David Swarbrick, director of marketing for Larousse, publishers of the dictionary, should result in an award to the Duchess of York and David Mellor for services to the English language. It means 'the practice of sucking a partner's toes for sexual stimulation'.

Lexicography has become a trendy business. Few publishers now maintain any pretence about restricting entries to words that have entered the 'core language', and the criterion of 'established usage' has come to mean whatever a publisher cares to bung in.

Only a year ago, the latest edition of the *Shorter Oxford English Dictionary* included 4,000 new words, including 'Majorism' and 'dweeb' (boringly conventional person). Three months later the 20-volume OED published two supplements containing an extra 6,000 words, including 'himbo' (male equivalent of bimbo), 'herstory' (history emphasising the role of women) and 'gobsmacked' (astounded).

Mr Swarbrick and Robert Allen, editor of the new Chambers dictionary, have resisted himbo and herstory but allowed dweeb. Himbo was a non-starter, they reckon. Even bimbos have become obsolete. 'Toy boy' has stuck, though now it is used tongue-in-cheek. They approve of 'gobsmacked'. As for 'Ramboesque', in a Collins dictionary: 'It should never have been there,' said Mr Swarbrick. 'Some dictionaries will publish any word that swings.'

Whether a neologism has staying power depends a lot on whether it can be freed from its origins for use in a generalised way. 'Glasnost' never came to mean openness outside the Russian context. 'Yomping', popularised during the Falklands war, never entered civilian language. Tabloid terms tend to be short-lived. But 'feelgood' will probably stay, as long as optimistic economic forecasts fail to produce optimism.

Oddly, the earliest British dictionaries, like today's, set out to list new words rather than champion the purity of the language. In Shakespeare's day, most dictionaries were slim glossaries containing words to do with, say, the leather trade. Cawdrey's dictionary of the early 17th century and Bailey's of the 18th were bought by people who wanted to find out the latest new words. It was Dr Johnson, whose memory is heartily reviled by Mr Allen, who tried to put a stop to that.

'He saw the dictionary as a means of fixing the language. But lexicographers should not be legislators. I don't sit in judgement on words. If they have achieved reasonable use they go in, whether they are offensive, taboo, funny or serious. I always resist pressure to champion 'pure language', the sort of thing the Queen's English Society stands for. It's an illusion. 'Standard English' is what is acceptable to people in power. It is a sociopolitical, not a linguistic thing. Monstrous.'

Which is why 'sexploitation', 'date rape', 'the munchies' (drug or alcohol-induced craving for food), 'social cleansing' and 'speciesism' have all found their way into his dictionary. All these are behaviour words springing from social change or fresh insights into social change, the sort that pre-Johnsonian lexicographers would have seized upon.

Assignment

◆ Having read both of the articles below, you are moved to write to your local newspaper because you can see that this difficult issue is riddled with complexity. In your letter you should address both sides of the argument in a balanced manner, in order to illustrate that there is no simple answer to the issue.

◆ Compare some aspects of your letter with one of the original texts. How did you make your letter different from its source? Concentrate on three areas for comment.

Text 5

THE KILLING FIELDS
(from 'Vendors' Voice' in *The Big Issue* October 1999)

Fox hunting has been a tradition in the United Kingdom for the last thousand years. It's been called the 'Sport of Kings'.

But should it stay? Hunting with hounds is barbaric and inhumane. Oscar Wilde famously described it as 'the unspeakable in full pursuit of the uneatable'.

More to the point, is it necessary? Hunting and killing foxes with hounds is a sport.

It's not about countryside management; it's not about farmers' incomes; nor is it about the availability of lamb chops on our plate. Even National Farmers' Union (NFU) figures reveal fewer than one in 200 lambs fall prey to foxes, while between 10 per cent and 24 per cent die of hypothermia, malnutrition and disease. Foxes then become ideal scapegoats for bad husbandry and lazy shepherds: Dead lambs?

But if you are lucky enough to see a fox in the fields, it is almost certainly scavenging for 'natural', already-dead casualties, not targeting healthy animals.

As the Ministry of Agriculture, Farming and Fisheries (MAFF) states: 'The predation of lambs by foxes is insignificant.'

At one time the fox had a natural predator: the wolf. But with the wolf hunted to extinction 300 years ago, the fox population soared, and were in turn targeted by the hunters. However, with improved breeding of both horses and hounds their figures soon fell significantly enough for the hunters to actually import foxes to kill.

Today in Britain 215,000 people participate in fox hunting each year. There are 185 fox-hunting packs in England and Wales, nine in Scotland and six Fell Packs and the activity generates £243m trade. According to a Countryside Alliance spokesman: 'There are 910 full-time jobs in hunt kennels, and another 14,000 jobs in related areas.'

The pro-hunting lobby claims that many of these jobs will be lost if Labour's proposed Bill (Wild Mammals, Hunting with Dogs) is passed, although Tony Blair's attitude appears to have cooled regarding banning fox hunting recently.

We cannot possibly need 15,000 people to manage the fox population, a sentiment shared by the National Fox Welfare Society (NFWS). 'Foxes do not carry keys or wire-cutters and will not enter a secure enclosure,' says an NFWS spokeswoman. 'Foxes do not need controlling, they are self-regulating.'

Fox hunting is a sport, so keep the sport, but get rid of the brutality. Drag hunting is a viable alternative. When drag hunting, the hounds follow an artificial scent. It is the same as fox hunting, but the fox is not used, and not killed. The hunters can keep all the traditional aspects of the sport simply by using this humane alternative.

To say 15,000 jobs are under threat is just not true. The drag hunter needs the same services and products as the fox hunter.

It's time to stop the brutality. Killing animals for pleasure is simply not acceptable in this day and age.

Text 6

HUNTING IN THE 21st CENTURY
(from the introduction to a booklet published by the Countryside Alliance)

For several hundred years, hunting has been an integral and important part of the fabric of social and rural life in Britain. However, we all know and understand the threats that now face it.

Hunting is a humane and natural method of controlling certain species and, as independent research shows, it is often the one method most favoured by farmers. The beneficial part it plays in the conservation of the countryside and the rural economy is beyond doubt.

In recent years urbanisation, as well as the proliferation of pressure groups, has sometimes led to misunderstanding and criticism of hunting. It is therefore the duty of those who take part to explain, inform and educate about what we do and why we do it.

There are over 300 packs of hounds in the UK hunting anywhere between 2 and 4 days a week *during the seasons*. Everyone involved in hunting must be conscious and sensitive to the fact that their activities are observed and judged by the public. We must be prepared to be held accountable for everything we do throughout each hunting day.

All hunting is regulated by strict and detailed rules laid down by the various

Governing Bodies, for hunt officials to observe. The standard of behaviour of followers whether on foot, in a car, or on a horse, has long been governed by an informal code. Those who run and manage hunting are fully conscious that if it is to flourish, then the highest standards need to be maintained, and understood by all followers.

For this reason, hunting's conventions, and the responsibilities of its followers, are now set down in this code. Follow it carefully and hunting will be available for future generations.

There are three golden rules at the heart of hunting's regulatory code:

◆ Hunting as a practice is the hunting of a wild animal in its wild and natural state. Nothing must be done which in any way compromises this precept.
◆ Hunting depends entirely on the goodwill of farmers. No-one who goes hunting should do anything that jeopardises that goodwill. It must be remembered that for all of a day's hunting you are the guest on someone else's property.
◆ Masters of Hounds (i.e. those in charge of the hunt) or their appointed deputies, are solely responsible for the conduct of the day's hunting and are bound by the strict rules and instructions from their Governing Body. Their authority is absolute and their instructions must be willingly obeyed.

Assignment

◆ The following two reviews are for a set of 20 Compact Discs, collectively entitled 'The Voice of the People', which can be bought as a set or as individual CDs. The first review comes from Q magazine, a general adult publication, the second from Folk Roots, a much more specialist magazine which devoted a whole page to the release of these CDs. Using these two reviews, write an entry for an Encyclopaedia of Compact Discs which gives information about the set and also public reaction at the time of the CDs' release. You are limited to 400 words; you do *not* need to write out the name of each CD; this will form part of the beginning of the encyclopaedia entry, which is not part of your remit. The names are given purely for your information.
◆ In what ways did you choose to write your entry? How have you conveyed your information? How does it compare to the source material?

Text 7

GREAT, BRITAIN
(from Q magazine)

It would probably be easier to scale the greased sides of Everest in carpet slippers than to persuade more than a handful of the British public of the pleasures to be had in their own traditional music. The Voice Of The People probably won't change any of that. Yet the sheer size and scholarly leanings of this venture constitute something of a landmark.

Compiled by scholar/musician Reg Hall, these 480 recordings have been grouped thematically into 20 stand-alone volumes. Each comes annotated with an introductory essay, complete lyrics and fascinating pen portraits of those involved. Men like Pop Maynard, Sam Larner and Jumbo Brightwell were born when Victoria reigned and were 'discovered' and recorded during the '50s, '60s and '70s when their voices were shaky with age, yet dignified and uncontaminated by outside influence. They and dozens like them here were the last links to a peasantry yoked for generations to the land. They had the songs to prove it: about work, sex, drink and death, just as it had been for hundreds of years.

Historically, each CD has its own merits. Yet particularly notable are the Ranting & Reeling collection which draws on a rich Northumbrian heritage and is full of wonderful playing, and the selections dedicated to tragic tales and songs of emigration (Volumes 3 and 4), ideal for those who like to wallow in the joy of despair, although the sound of Morris men whacking their sticks and jingling their bells is probably one bridge too far.

In fact, those discs where the emphasis is on pageantry (Volumes 9 and 16) and jollity (7 and 14) turn out to be the least appealing. Mostly, as with some of the 17th Volume's longer ballads like *What Put The Blood?* and *Lord Baker*, there are traces of a world that's now largely gone but, thanks to this splendid series, not forgotten.

Text 8

(from Folk Roots magazine)

This goes way, way beyond music. 20 thematic anthologies, involving 500 largely rare recordings of the singers and musicians who've provided the essential backbone of traditional British and Irish folk song through the last century. Culturally, socially and historically, it is quite simply the most important set of releases any of us are likely to see in our lifetimes.

The credit due to Topic, notably its main architects Tony Engle and Reg Hall, is immeasurable. It's one thing to be vaguely aware of the source singers who carried the torch for our indigenous music through many decades of disdain and indifference, and quite another to have them presented in such a proud and attractive manner, enabling them to assume their rightful place in the roll call of the century. From Paddy Tunney to Margaret Barry, Bob Hart to Walter Pardon, Harry Cox to Jeannie Robertson, Pop Maynard to Fred Jordan, these do indeed represent a true Voice Of The People, and as such merit the same reverence reserved for great classical composers, jazz musicians or pop performers. Providing beautiful packaging and a superb 62-page booklet with each collection, Topic is unlikely to make a profit from such an ambitious venture, but has placed its responsibilities to the tradition above all commercial considerations and this is itself a reflection of the humbling nature of these collections. We can but doff our cap to the artists represented and fall to our knees in gratitude that the keeper of their flame is a company determined to see them as a living, breathing inspiration to successive generations rather than an antique museum piece. It's hardly bearable to imagine the consequences had it ended up under the inert control of those still sitting on some of the wonderful revival material directly resulting from some of these original recordings.

Much of the material comes from Topic's own archive and you imagine there must have been many long and hard discussions about the most effective way of reactivating it. They've got it spot on. The mix'n'match approach ensures constant variety, emphasising the individuality of the artists, and in sociological terms the songs paint an enthralling picture of the attitude, manner and character of the times through the differing themes of the anthologies. In their entirety the songs of courtship and marriage, emigration, farming, gypsies, the sea, seasonal events, hunting and poaching, tragedy, drinking and work represent aural snapshots of everyday life at work and play and that, surely, is the truest and most valuable function of folk music.

More than that – *much* more than that – the whole series stands alone as great music: without any qualification or recourse to intellectual justification. One of the considerable achievements of the accompanying booklets and Reg Hall's magnificent notes is to make the performers real and human. Phil Tanner and Harry Cox aren't distant, anonymous legends any more – they're real and they're here and Topic make a decent fist of making them relevant and enriching. They go beyond the reach of worthy academia to give the music an enticing showcase where it can be absorbed and enjoyed in its own context on its own merits. Given that release from murky archives, it is moving, charming, provocative and, yes, even thrilling. It's impossible to listen to Percy Grainger's 1908 cylinder recording of Joseph Taylor singing *The Gypsy Girl* (from *Come Let Us Buy The License*) and not feel a rush of excitement, furthered by parallel memories of Shirley Collins' electrified landmark *No Roses* update over six decades later (a sense of osmosis also incurred by Pop Maynard's *Just As The Tide Was Flowing*). The License CD is especially strong – amassing other legends like the Gower farmer Phil Tanner (a blissful *Sweet Primroses*), Pop Maynard (an emotive *Our Captain Cried All Hounds*), Harry Cox (a persuasive *The Sold Fisherman*), Jeannie Robertson (with a sprightly *An Old Man Came Courting Me*) and Sussex flower seller, Mary Ann Haynes, singing *Lovely Johnny*. Haynes in fact turns out to be a constantly invigorating presence across the entire anthology.

FOR INFORMATION AND REFERENCE ONLY

The 20 titles in the series are:

Volume 1: Come Let Us Buy The License – Songs of Courtship & Marriage

Volume 2: My Ship Shall Sail The Ocean – Songs of Tempest, Sea Battles, Sailor Lads & Fishermen

Volume 3: O'er His Grave The Grass Grew Green – Tragic Ballads

Volume 4: Farewell, My Dear Native Land – Songs Of Exile & Emigration

Volume 5: Come All My Lads That Follow The Plough – The Life Of Rural Working Men & Women

Volume 6: Tonight I'll Make You My Bride – Ballads Of True & False Lovers

Volume 7: First I'm Going To Sing You A Ditty – Rural Fun & Frolics

Volume 8: A Story I'm Just About To Tell – Local Events & National Issues

Volume 9: Rig-A-Jig-Jig – Dance Music In The South Of England

Volume 10: Who's That At My Bed Window? – Songs Of Love & Amorous Encounters

Volume 11: My Father's The King Of The Gypsies – Music Of English & Welsh Travellers

Volume 12: We've Received Orders To Sail – Jackie Tar At Sea & On Shore

Volume 13: They Ordered Their Pints Of Bitter & Bottles Of Sherry – The Joys & Curse Of Drink

Volume 14: Troubles They Are But Few – Dance Tunes & Ditties

Volume 15: As Me & My Love Sat Courting – Songs Of Love & Courtship

Volume 16: You Lazy Lot Of Bone Shakers – Songs & Dance Tunes Of Seasonal Events

Volume 17: It Fell On A Bonny Sunny Day – Ballads

Volume 18: To Catch A Fine Buck Was My Delight – Songs Of Hunting & Poaching

Volume 19: Ranting & Reeling – Dance Music Of The North Of England

Volume 20: There Is A Man Upon The Farm – Working Men & Women In Song.

Examination assignment

Question 1

Read the following three extracts from books, which are all on the topic of 'the English people'. Imagine you have been researching attitudes to English people as represented in quality writing, and you have to reply to the criticisms being made by writing a short but pithy article of your own for a national newspaper. The article will be entitled: *Are we really that bad?*

Using some of the source material printed below, write your article in no more than 400 words.

Question 2

Write a critical analysis of your article by comparing it with one of the original sources. You should concentrate on your purpose and the way you used language to help meet your purpose.

Text A

This extract is taken from Jeremy Paxman's book *The English*.

England's national day, 23 April, passes mostly unnoticed, while invented *British* ceremonial events like 'the Queen's official birthday' (her what?) are marked by artillery salutes, flag-flying and parties at British embassies around the world. The closest thing the English have to a national dance, Morris-dancing, is a clumsy pub-sport practised by men in beards and shiny-bottomed trousers. When the English play Wales or Scotland at soccer or rugby, the Scots have 'Flower of Scotland' to sing, the Welsh, 'Land of My Fathers'. The English team must mouth along with the *British* national anthem, that dirge-like glorification of the monarchy whose job it is to unite the disparate parts of an increasingly tattered political union. At the Commonwealth Games the organizers have adopted 'Land of Hope and Glory' as the English anthem.

There are over 500 other distinctly Scottish songs, many of which are widely known: go into an English pub and ask for a verse of 'There'll always be an England', 'The Yeomen of England' or any other of the old national songs and you will be met with baffled silence. Or worse. The only song an English sports crowd can manage with any enthusiasm is the slave spiritual 'Swing Low, Sweet Chariot' at rugby matches, and a few superannuated pop songs, often with obscene lyrics, at soccer games.

What does this paucity of national symbols mean? You could argue that it demonstrates a certain self-confidence. No English person can look at the swearing of allegiance that takes place in American schools every day without feeling bewilderment: that sort of public declaration of patriotism seems so, well, naive. When an Irishman wears a bunch of shamrock on St Patrick's Day, the English look on with patronizing indulgence: scarcely anyone sports a rose on St George's Day. This worldly wisdom soon elides into a general view that any public display of national pride is not merely unsophisticated but somehow morally reprehensible. George Orwell noticed it as long ago as 1948 when he wrote that:

In left-wing circles it is always felt that there is something slightly disgraceful in being an Englishman, and that it is a duty to snigger at every English institution, from horse-racing to suet puddings. It is a strange fact, but it is unquestionably true, that almost any English intellectual would feel more ashamed of standing to attention during 'God Save the King' than of stealing from a poor box.

No one stands for 'God Save the Queen' any more, and any cinema manager who tried to revive the custom of playing the national anthem would find the place empty before he'd reached the end of the first verse. At the time of Orwell's

Jeremy Paxman, BBC presenter and author of The English

irritation, left-wing intellectual disdain was cheap because the English didn't need to concern themselves with the symbols of their own identity: when you're top dog in the world's leading empire, you don't need to. And since 'Britain' was essentially a political invention, it was necessary to submerge the identities of the constituent parts of the United Kingdom within it. The beleaguered tribe of Protestant settlers transplanted to the north of Ireland clung to the British identity fiercely because they had nothing else, but in other places on the Celtic fringe, traditional identities could easily co-exist with being British, a fact the English were happy to acknowledge, since it rather proved the Union was what they said it was, a Union of distinct places. Hence, the nicknames: Scots are Jocks, Welshmen Taffies and Irishmen Paddies or Micks, but – another sign of their dominance – it is noticeable there is no similar designation for the English.

Text B

This extract comes from American writer Bill Bryson's book *Notes From A Small Island.*

There are certain things that you have to be British or at least older than me, or possibly both, to appreciate: Sooty, Tony Hancock, *Bill and Ben the Flowerpot Men*, Marmite, skiffle music, that *Morecambe and Wise* segment in which Angela Rippon shows off her legs by dancing, Gracie Fields singing 'Sally', George Formby doing anything, *Dixon of Dock Green*, HP sauce, salt cellars with a single large hole, travelling fun fairs, making sandwiches from bread you've sliced yourself, really milky tea, allotments, the belief that household wiring is an interesting topic for conversation, steam trains, toast made under a gas grill, thinking that going to choose wallpaper with your mate constitutes a reasonably good day out, wine made out of something other than grapes, unheated bedrooms and bathrooms, seaside rock, erecting windbreaks on a beach (why, pray, are you *there* if you need a windbreak?) and taking an interest in by-elections. There may be one or two others that don't occur to me at the moment. I'm not saying that these things are bad or boring or misguided, merely that their full value and appeal yet eludes me.

Text C

Jonathan Raban wrote the final extract; at the time he was travelling around the coast of Britain in a yacht.

The Roman poet Virgil, one of the earliest foreign observers, wrote that 'Britons are wholly sundered from all the world'. They're famous for their insular arrogance and condescension. They love fine social distinctions and divisions and are snobbishly wedded to an antique system of caste and class. Yet the upper lips of this superior race are so notoriously stiff that they can barely bring themselves to speak, preferring to communicate in monosyllables interleaved with gruff silences. They are aggressively practical and philistine, with a loud contempt for anything that smells abstract or theoretical. They are a nation of moneygrubbers and bargain-hunters, treasuring pennies for treasuring's sake. When the English reach for a superlative to praise someone for his general moral excellence, they say he has a 'sterling character', meaning that he has some of the same quality as the coins which they like to chink noisily in their pockets.

When it comes to sex, they are furtive and hypocritical – and their erotic tastes are known to be extremely peculiar. Many Englishmen will pay a woman money to take their trousers down and spank them. Others cultivate a neoclassical passion for small boys – preferably boys of a lower caste or another colour. For the most part, though, the English, both men and women, are afflicted by such a morbid decay of the libido that it has always puzzled the rest of the world how the English manage to reproduce themselves at all.

They are casually rude – a vice which they claim as a virtue by labelling it as forthrightness. They are also violent; feared in all the neighbouring countries of Europe for the marauding hooligans who accompany their football teams and sometimes murder spectators who have come to cheer a rival side. In compensation, however, they are soft-hearted about animals, for which they have an arsenal of sentimental nicknames, like 'pooches', 'bunnies', 'pussies' and 'feathered friends'. Yet they enjoy dressing up in ceremonial outfits to go round the country on horseback setting packs of dogs on foxes. When the fox has been dismembered, it is the English custom to smear the faces of little girls with its blood. This sport is a favourite subject with the artists who design English Christmas cards.

Student response

<u>Question 1</u>

Are We Really That Bad?

The English, it would seem, have somehow gained a reputation of being a nation of boring, arrogant, xenophobic megalomaniacs. Quite why this has come about is difficult to understand; the English have been for a long time, and continue to be, a nationality respected the world over, for their culture, their educational system, and their power as a trade ally.

→

Why else would the English language be so widely spoken, and why else would the nouveau riche, the world over, send their children to be educated in our schools?

We are often accused of having a lack of national symbols, or if not a deficiency, then symbols which inspire merely mirth or confusion; Morris dancing, for example. But then does *anyone* really know what that is all about? True, national events such as the Queen's official birthday do seem archaic and mildly confusing; after all, why should she, and no-one else, get two birthdays? However, it is the very quaintness of these traditions that should make us proud to be English. They are as much a part of our heritage as thatched cottages, London buses and sandy sandwiches on the beach. Imagine an England without these things, and you are imagining almost a different world. One must also think about the trade in tourism that they provide; without them we would lose all those Americans who come here with only those things in mind (actually, now I think about this more closely, maybe we would be better off . . . no, I digress . . .) The point is that, although these things are faintly embarrassing, like an elderly aunt who smells slightly damp, they are part of our Englishness, and it needs to be remembered that there always will be, as long as England remains English, a man who insists on prancing about with bells on his shoes, waving two hankies.

Certain pastimes and recreations considered typically English are often sources of confusion and indeed laughter, for those of a not-so-English persuasion. Obsessing about the weather, for example, Tony Hancock, days out at the seaside, George Formby: the list could be endless. However, nowadays, especially amongst the younger generations of English people, (who have had the joy of being subjected to Tony Blair's not-so-cool-'Cool Britannia' campaign), we view these things with more than a hint of irony. Yes, these things are often crass, pointless and more than likely stupid, but they are undeniably *English*, and outsiders should be impressed that the youth of England has managed to get an angle on (albeit with their tongues lodged firmly in their cheeks) their sense of national pride once more.

Everyone in the world is a 'national stereotype', everyone has helped form those stereotypes, even from that minor event that might have happened to you in Barbados last year. No one can help it; it is human nature to create images of nationalities and sometimes to live up (or down) to them as well. The English are not the only race subject to this phenomenon and we have no right to complain, either; how many times have you told the joke about the German and the beach towels, or the French waiter and the frogs legs? I rest my case.

What we should bear in mind is that as English people who live in a global community, we are all, every one of us, ambassadors for England.

→

We must look into the reasons *why* these stereotypes have arisen – the football hooligans and the arrogant holidaymakers who think that 'speaking the lingo' involves merely shouting loudly and slowly at the waiter – and attempt to remedy them. Then maybe we really would be 'Cool Britannia'.

Question 2

The question states that the article is to be a reply to criticisms made in the selections and that it should be aimed at the audience who might read a national newspaper. In terms of style, this means that the language should be reasonably sophisticated. However, we are not told whether the newspaper would be a tabloid or a broadsheet. Therefore I feel that the language should be kept within a certain domain to ensure that the article is accessible to the readers of both types of newspapers.

In my own article I attempted to make the language lie in a plane somewhere between Jeremy Paxman's and Bill Bryson's. These two authors, in my opinion, have the kind of language which is most accessible to an audience on a general scale, whereas Raban's language seems to be on a more intellectual level, which would probably have the effect of alienating the audience, particularly a tabloid readership.

The three selections focus on three areas of Englishness, criticizing them in terms of their pointlessness. In my article, my purpose became that of answering these criticisms, defending the focus of the three extracts, and if not actually offering any remedies for any problems, then at least drawing a cohesive conclusion from my own article. Since the three extracts look at English traditions, English pastimes, and English attitudes, it made sense to address these areas in my article.

For instance, in Paxman's article he addresses the reader through use of rhetorical questions such as: 'What does this paucity of national symbols mean?' In my article I also used this device, but in a quite different manner: 'Why else would the English language be so widely spoken, and why else would the nouveau riche, the world over, send their children to be educated in our schools?'

Whereas Paxman uses the question to draw together the issues he has already addressed in the previous paragraph, my question opens out the issue of Englishness in a positive manner, thus providing a base of the rest of the article. Similarly, my question: 'Morris dancing, for example. But then does *anyone* really know what that is all about?' is used to inject some humour into the article and appeal to a younger section of the audience by utilizing a phrase commonly used in the spoken mode to express utter speechlessness about an event's existence.

Paxman uses adjectives in a fairly frugal manner: 'clumsy', 'obscene' and 'general' are three examples of premodifiers that he uses in the body of

→

this article. However, I made a conscious effort to use adjectives in tightly packaged bundles to increase the potency of the noun phrase that follows. For instance, I use: 'a nation of boring, arrogant, xenophobic megalomaniacs', where the pattern of three adjectives helps to intensify, as well as conflate, the views that are expressed in the articles. Later in my article I use the same structural device when I say: '. . . as much part of our heritage as thatched cottages, London buses and sandy sandwiches on the beach', where the pattern utilizes three premodified nouns in sequence to once again accentuate the nature of essential Englishness.

Paxman uses adverbs quite liberally in his article in a way that helps to focus the manner of his feelings: 'fiercely', 'mostly' and 'essentially'. I chose to lessen the impact of what Paxman was saying by using much weaker adverbs: 'mildly', 'slightly' and 'faintly'. Whilst not antonyms of the previously mentioned adverbs, these adverbs do help the overall cohesion of my article, by heightening the positive nature of what I am saying.

The overall tone that I took in my own article was one of tongue-in-cheek humour, as it seemed to me that this was the tone that matched those of the extracts best. Both Paxman's and Bryson's extract are humorous, Paxman's in a sarcastic manner and Bryson's in a placidly amusing yet confused way. Jonathan Raban's piece also uses humour, but a much stronger satirical humour, and I decided to avoid this kind of language in my own article, as it can not only alienate part of the audience (satire is a form of humour which you either understand and appreciate, or you just don't), but if it is taken seriously, it can also offend. I stuck to the kind of gently humorous language that involves personal asides to the reader, emulating Paxman's style of using parenthetical phrases.

All three extracts use specific examples to demonstrate their points. Bill Bryson uses long lists with the purpose of being amusing, Jeremy Paxman targets humour, although he does not use long lists in his examples, and Jonathan Raban's extract is a collection of paragraphs made up of very verbose lists! In my article I attempted to combine the two techniques, by giving short lists as examples, with the aim of being humorous. Hopefully this type of language would prevent the target audience from becoming bored with long lists of things, and it would amuse them and illustrate my points at the same time. ◆

Examiner's comments

This answer is both interesting and well written. In the first question, the student uses a good deal of source material and individualizes it; to check how much of the original articles are used, simply go through the student answer and cross reference the factual material inserted into the article with the original sources. The article that the student has produced is well structured, has a clear direction and is cogently written. The student uses a number of techniques to help the thrust of the article, which are then picked out and discussed in the comparative commentary: she discusses the use of adjectives, adverbs and rhetorical questions, thus satisfying the terms of the question. In the exam, there will be little time to discuss more than three specific examples in the commentary. The student talks in more general terms about audience, which she leaves deliberately vague. She could have been a little more specific here and selected a particular type of newspaper, which would have resulted in a more targeted article and a tighter commentary.

Nonetheless, this is a very good article and a thorough commentary, which would attract high marks overall.

8 Language in Context: The Synoptic Paper

Introduction

The final paper you will take in the A2 part of the course tests your ability to draw together all aspects of your combined literary and linguistic study, by giving you a variety of texts to analyse comparatively. A literary text, a non-literary text and a spontaneous speech act will always be included in these questions, and there will always be some kind of link between the three texts.

It is entirely up to you how you tackle the comparison, but you should always have your framework for analysis clearly mapped out, since the second part of the question will ask you to focus on the methodology you adopted for your critical comparison.

You will find four practice papers below, the last of which has a student answer followed by an examiner's critique.

Practice Paper 1

Question 1

Read the following three texts. Examine the ways that each of the writers and speakers convey their feelings in their texts, comparing the suitability of each mode and form for their specific purpose.

Question 2

What methods did you choose when examining these texts? Evaluate how useful you found them in helping you to understand and respond to each of the texts.

Text A

In the following piece of speech an inmate of a prison recounts an experience she had whilst imprisoned.

Transcription key:

(.)	a micropause
(1.0)	a pause of one second

.h	intake of breath
::	elongated sound

full stop after letters, eg: tr. (line 18): a word started but not completed.
(Some words have been spelt to represent their pronunciation.)

I can remember being in Holloway (.) and erm (.) I didn't know (.) that I was
having a visit an' my children .h come running along an' .h of course you know (.)
natural you're gonna run and pick them up they're running along in the prison I
was quite (.) couldn't believe it (.) so off we went we all walked together to the
probation area then afterwards .h there were about six or seven officers there (.)
screws (.) and they said erin (0.5) I can't I have to wait there in this room .h and
my (.) children had made me this calendar at school where they had stuck like bits
of erm .h wheat and (.) pasta and things like that on it and glitter and things like
that and I had in my hand .h an::d they took me up to security to to to a search
place .h an::d (.) this officer erm just ripped this calendar to pieces (1.0) because
they'd been brought in the prison the children and I'd seen them (.) before::
they'd been escorted properly into the room so that I had access to them (.) they
saw that as a security that they could have bought anythink into me .h and that
was it (.) I just flipped (.) I went mad and I was held down and injections stuck in
you and (1.0) that was the beginning of quite a number of weeks of tr. re.
rebelling erm coz I was just horrified I wasn't g. I wasn't going to have that no my
children made me that

Text B

The following text was first printed in *The Mail on Sunday* and was written
by Bill Bryson while living in America and writing weekly for his British
audience.

YOUR NEW COMPUTER

Congratulations. You have purchased an Anthrax/2000 Multimedia 615X Personal
Computer with Digital Doo-Dah Enhancer. It will give years of faithful service, if
you ever get it up and running. Also included with your PC is a bonus pack of
pre-installed software – 'Lawn Mowing Planner', 'Mr Arty-Farty', 'Blank Screen
Save', and 'East Africa Route Finder' – which will provide hours of pointless
diversion while using up most of your computer's spare memory. So turn the
page and let's get started!

Getting ready: Congratulations. You have successfully turned the page and are
ready to proceed.
Important meaningless note: The Anthrax/2000 is configured to use 80386,
214J10 or higher processors running at 2,472 hertz on variable speed spin cycle.
Check your electrical installations and insurance policies before proceeding. Do
not tumble dry.

To prevent internal heat build-up, select a cool, dry environment for your
computer. The bottom shelf of a refrigerator is ideal.

Unpack the box and examine its contents. (Warning. Do not open box if contents are missing or faulty as this will invalidate your warranty. Return all missing contents in their original packaging with a note explaining where they have gone and a replacement will be sent within twelve working months.)

The contents of the box should include some of the following: monitor with mysterious De Gauss button; keyboard with 2½ inches of flex; computer unit; miscellaneous wires and cables not necessarily designed for this model; 2,000-page *Owner's Manual*; *Short Guide to the Owner's Manual*; *Quick Guide to the Short Guide to the Owner's Manual*; *Laminated Super-Kwik Set-Up Guide for People Who Are Exceptionally Impatient or Stupid*; 1,167 pages of warranties, vouchers, notices in Spanish, and other loose pieces of paper; 292 cubic feet of styrofoam packing material.

Something They Didn't Tell You in the Shop: Because of the additional power needs of the pre-installed bonus software, you will need to acquire an Anthrax/2000 auxiliary software upgrade pack, a 900-volt memory capacitator for the auxiliary software pack, a 50-megaherz oscillator unit for the memory capacitator, 2,500 mega-gigabytes of additional memory for the oscillator, and an electrical substation.

Setting Up: Congratulations. You are ready to set up. If you have not yet acquired a degree in electrical engineering, now is the time to do so.

Connect the monitor cable (A) to the portside outlet unit (D); attach power offload unit sub-orbiter (Xii) to the co-axial AC/DC servo channel (G); plug three-pin mouse cable into keyboard housing unit (make extra hole if necessary); connect modem (B2) to offside parallel audio/video lineout jack. Alternatively, plug the cables into the most likely looking holes, switch on and see what happens.

Additional important meaningless note: the wires in the ampule modulator unit are marked as follows according to international convention: blue = neutral or live; Yellow = live or blue; blue and live = neutral and green; black = instant death. (Except where prohibited by law.)

Switch your computer on. Your hard drive will automatically download. (Allow three to five days.) When downloading is complete, your screen will say: 'Yeah, what?'

Text C

The following poem is by Simon Armitage.

VERY SIMPLY TOPPING UP THE BRAKE FLUID

Yes, love, that's why the warning light comes on. Don't
panic. Fetch some universal brake-fluid
and a five-eighths screwdriver from your toolkit
then prop the bonnet open. Go on, it won't

eat you. Now, without slicing through the fan-belt
try and slide the sharp end of the screwdriver
under the lid and push the spade connector
through its bed, go on, that's it. Now you're all right

to unscrew, no, clockwise, you see it's Russian
love, back to front, that's it. You see, it's empty.
Now, gently with your hand and I mean gently,
try and create a bit of space by pushing

the float-chamber sideways so there's room to pour,
gently does it, that's it. Try not to spill it, it's
corrosive: rusts, you know, and fill it till it's
level with the notch on the clutch reservoir.

Lovely. There's some Swarfega in the office
if you want a wash and some soft roll above
the cistern for, you know. Oh don't mind him, love,
he doesn't bite. Come here and sit down Prince. Prince!

Now, where's that bloody alternator? Managed?
Oh any time, love. I'll not charge you for that
because it's nothing of a job. If you want
us again we're in the book. Tell your husband.

Practice Paper 2

Question 1

Read the following three texts very carefully. Each one recounts an accident of some kind.

Compare the way language is used in each text and the effects that are intended by each of the writers or speakers. You should pay special attention to the way that purpose and audience are addressed in each text.

Question 2

What methods did you use to compare these three texts? How useful did you find your particular method in helping you to interpret the texts?

Text A

In the following extract from *The Child in Time* the main character, Stephen, is involved in a road accident.

Stephen was driving a hired car along a deserted minor road, eastwards towards central Suffolk. The sunroof was open wide. He had tired of searching for tolerable music on the radio and was content with the rush of warm air and the novelty of driving for the first time in over a year. The sun was high behind him, giving a visibility of luminous clarity. The road was flanked by concrete irrigation ditches and made wide curves through miles of conifer plantation set well back beyond a wide swathe of tree stumps and dried out bracken. He had slept well the night before, he remembered later. He was relaxed but reasonably alert. His speed was somewhere between seventy and seventy-five, which dropped only a little as he came up behind a large pink lorry.

In what followed, the rapidity of events was accommodated by the slowing of time. He was preparing to overtake when something happened – he did not quite see what – in the region of the lorry's wheels, a hiatus, a cloud of dust, and then, something black and long snaked through a hundred feet towards him. It slapped the windscreen, clung there a moment and was whisked away before he had time to understand what it was. And then – or did this happen in the same moment? – the rear of the lorry made a complicated set of movements, a bouncing and swaying, and slewed in a wide spray of sparks, bright even in sunshine. Something curved and metallic flew off to one side. So far Stephen had had time to move his foot towards the brake, time to notice a padlock swinging on a loose flange, and 'Wash me please' scrawled in grime. There was a whinnying of scraped metal and new sparks, dense enough to form a white flame which seemed to propel the rear of the lorry into the air. He was applying first pressure to the brake as he saw the dusty, spinning wheels, the oily bulge of the differential, the camshaft, and now, at eye level, the base of the gear box. The upended lorry bounced on its nose once, perhaps twice, then lazily, tentatively, began to complete the somersault, bringing Stephen the inverted radiator grill, the downward flash of windscreen and a deep boom as the roof hit the road, rose again several feet, fell back, and surged along before him on a bed of flame. Then it swung its length round to block the road, fell on to its side and stopped abruptly as Stephen headed into it from a distance of less than a hundred feet and at a speed which he estimated, in a detached kind of way, to be forty-five miles an hour.

Now, in this slowing of time, there was a sense of a fresh beginning. He had entered a much later period in which all the terms and conditions had changed. So these were the new rules, and he experienced something like awe, as though he were walking alone into a great city on a newly discovered planet. There was space too for a little touch of regret, genuine nostalgia for the old days of spectacle, back then when a lorry used to catapult so impressively before the impassive witness. Now was a more demanding time of effort and concentration. He was pointing the car towards a six-foot gap formed between a road sign and the front bumper of the motionless lorry. He had removed his foot from the brakes, reasoning – and it was as if he had just completed a monograph on the subject – that they were pulling the car to one side, interfering with his aim. Instead he was changing down through the gears and steering with both hands firmly, but not too tightly, on the wheel, ready to bring them up to cover his head if he missed. He beamed messages, or rather messages sprang from him, to Julie and Kate, nothing more distinct than pulses of alarm and love. There were others he should send to, he knew, but time was short, less than half a second, and fortunately they did not come to mind to confuse him. As he shifted to second and the small car gave out a protesting roar, it was clear that he must not think too hard, that he had to trust to a relaxed and dissociated thinking, that he must imagine himself into the gap. On the sound of this very word, which he must have spoken aloud, there was a brisk crunch of metal and glass and he was through and coming to a halt, with his door handle and wing mirror scattered across the road fifty feet behind.

Before the relief, before the shock, came an intense hope that the driver of the lorry had witnessed this feat of driving. Stephen sat motionless, still holding the steering wheel, watching himself through the eyes of the man in the vehicle behind. If not the driver, then a passer-by would do, some farmer perhaps, someone who understood driving and would have the full measure of his accomplishment. He wanted applause, he wanted a passenger in the front seat turning to him now with shining eyes.

Text B

A young Welshman tells of an accident he remembers as a child.

The tramlines . . . ah they used to have . . . erm from the pit there used to be a tramline right to the top o the mountain . . . used to work on a . . . a pulley sort of system I should think I was too young to know then. They used to have about fifteen to twenty big pit drams on this wire rope and I would say it must have stretched, bottom to top, about three and a half, maybe four miles, and of course we'd winch up on it, pulled up, cos all the kids would be running up, jumping on . . . and, er, I would say, well there was one boy, how old is Gevin . . . must be about thirty-eight he's . . . jumped on and he fell off and it cut his leg clean off. But they're big metal drams, they weighed well, they must weigh about a ton with nothing in them, so you can imagine when they're full . . . and of course when they come down the journey again . . . they're coming down at a fair speed cos they let them go down quite a bit and then they got them . . . on automatic brake, I think, and it slows them down . . . we used to come down there. We used to jump on them on the top and ride down . . . things you do when you're young . . . We'd always be warned – don't ride on the drams . . . straight down the bottom and wait for them to come up and you'd you'd run up along side them and just jump on . . . the most dangerous thing about that was . . . er . . . was the rope, the metal rope, which was about two inches in diameter, and it used to whip. And of course you imagine a steel rope whipping . . . well it'd cut a man clean in half . . . you never see the dangers when you're young, do you?

Text C

Gillian Moseley remembers her experience of being on the *Marchioness* riverboat when it was struck by the *Bowbelle* on the River Thames. Fifty-one people were killed in the disaster. The article was written for *Scotland on Sunday*.

It was six years ago this week, a Saturday night in August, that I was invited to a boat party on the Thames. The weather was perfect and we were excited about taking a midnight cruise along the Embankment. Hot summer parties on boats don't happen very often in Britain. The party was packed with twentysomethings and my friend Chris and I were intent on having a good time. The boat was the *Marchioness*.

After exploring the boat we spent some time in the bar drinking and eating. Four of us decided to go up to the main deck and check out the disco. It was crowded and the two friends who were leading the way went out on to the deck. I stopped to dance with Chris, we liked the song that was playing. It reminded us of Ibiza.

When the record skipped I laughed, I thought the DJ had made a mistake. Then there was a jolt. We turned to look through the window behind us. It looked like there was a black sheet next to the boat. Chris and I looked at each other in horror and lunged towards the door. We were six feet from it but there was no time to reach it. The floor was tilting downwards and the lights went out.

Within two seconds I was completely immersed in water, trapped inside the boat. I kept thinking, 'These things don't happen in real life, we'll all be fine. This is just a bad dream.' I was trying to paddle upwards while the people below me kept pulling at me. I wondered why they were grabbing at me trying to hoist themselves upwards, there was nowhere to go. It didn't even occur to me that I should try to find a window to climb out of. I was trapped in the boat.

Through my feelings of disbelief, came the realisation that this was actually happening. I thought: 'This is it.' Despite people continuing to claw at me the water was completely silent. It felt even tranquil; I couldn't hold my breath any longer. I resigned myself to my situation. I was feeling very light-headed and started seeing stars.

The Marchioness *riverboat disaster on the Thames cost 51 lives*

I had almost blacked out when I found myself in an air pocket. I hauled myself upwards and when I was halfway to the end of the 'wall', someone opened a hatch above me. I pulled myself out of it, stupefied. I was the first person out of the boat when it re-emerged after being rammed under water by the *Bowbelle*. I jumped and swam to a life raft a few feet away and sat soberly, wishing the girl on the life raft next to me would stop screaming. I wanted to scream myself but I was too shocked. Her screams were a horrible reminder of what we'd just been through.

My friend Chris died that night. I will never understand how we could have looked at each other as the *Bowbelle* struck, and then he died and I escaped. Everyone around me, including myself, was mourning his death. I think that kept me from absorbing what had just happened to me. I travelled for six months afterwards without being able to leave behind my recollections of my night on the *Marchioness*. I still haven't worked out why he died and I survived.

Practice Paper 3

Question 1

Read the following three texts. Compare how the writers and speakers represent their experiences with animals. You should make reference to:

◆ use of vocabulary
◆ narrative voice and attitude
◆ use of stylistic features
◆ any other matters you consider to be important.

Question 2

In what ways did you choose to compare these texts? To what extent did your methods help your overall response?

Text A

The following is an excerpt from *Snake*, a poem by D.H. Lawrence, written when he was in Sicily.

A snake came to my water-trough
On a hot, hot day, and I in pyjamas for the heat,
To drink there.

In the deep, strange-scented shade of the great dark carob-tree
I came down the steps with my pitcher
And must wait, must stand and wait, for there he was at the trough before me.

He reached down from a fissure in the earth-wall in the gloom
And trailed his yellow-brown slackness soft-bellied down, over the edge of the stone trough

And rested his throat upon the stone bottom,
And where the water had dripped from the tap, in a small clearness,
He sipped with his straight mouth,
Softly drank through his straight gums, into his slack long body,
Silently.

Someone was before me at my water-trough,
And I, like a second comer, waiting.

He lifted his head from his drinking, as cattle do,
And looked at me vaguely, as drinking cattle do,
And flickered his two-forked tongue from his lips, and mused a moment,
And stooped and drank a little more,
Being earth-brown, earth-golden from the burning bowels of the earth
On the day of Sicilian July, with Etna smoking.

The voice of my education said to me
He must be killed,
For in Sicily the black, black snakes are innocent, the gold are venomous.

And voices in me said, If you were a man
You would take a stick and break him now, and finish him off.

But must I confess how I liked him,
How glad I was he had come like a guest in quiet, to drink at my water-trough
And depart peaceful, pacified, and thankless,
Into the burning bowels of this earth?

Was it cowardice, that I dared not kill him?
Was it perversity, that I longed to talk to him?
Was it humility, to feel so honoured?
I felt so honoured.

And yet those voices:
If you were not afraid, you would kill him!

And truly I was afraid, I was most afraid,
But even so, honoured still more
That he should seek my hospitality
From out the dark door of the secret earth.

He drank enough
And lifted his head, dreamily, as one who has drunken,
And flickered his tongue like a forked night on the air, so black;
Seeming to lick his lips,
And looked around like a god, unseeing, into the air,
And slowly turned his head,
And slowly, very slowly, as if thrice adream,
Proceeded to draw his slow length curving round
And climb again the broken bank of my wall-face.

Text B

A boy recounts an incident that involved him and his family when they lived in Africa.

Key:

(.)   a pause

When I was a only as little boy I lived in Africa with my sister (.) and (.) Zimbabwe (.) we lived there for quite a while (.) about two years (.) till I was three and we came over to England (.) all (.) when I was about two (.) two and a half and my sister was three and a half (.) my mum and dad took us to (.) a party (.) and (.) it started rain (.) um it was outside because it's so hot inside so (.) and it started raining (.) and (.) it's the African rain (.) rainfall you know where it's it's steaming (.) streaming hot rain sort of thing (.) so (.) um (.) we ran home quick and I was in the pram (.) and my mum and dad went into the bedroom (.) just to see (.) see if everything was all right and (.) me and Samantha were in our cots (.) and (.) my dad looked (.) my Dad could hear crack (.) crackling echoing round the room so (.) it was like creaking or something and they were looking round and my mum said John (.) like this (.) and there was a (.) big blue and yellow spider about that big (.) on the ceiling (.) and my Dad panicked (.) he thought it might be poisonous so (.) it was like um (.) he got (.) he got my mum's high heel shoe and (.) ever so quickly (.) he walked up like this (.) and it moved and he jumped (.) he jumped back down (.) and it crawled all the way down the ceiling (.) mum (.) my mum was sort of like panicking and running out and um (.) he took a quick shot at it and got it in (.) the thing went straight through the spider

Text C

In this extract from *My Family and Other Animals*, Gerald Durrell examines a wall in his garden in Corfu, making some unusual discoveries.

The crumbling wall that surrounded the sunken garden alongside the house was a rich hunting ground for me. It was an ancient brick wall that had been plastered over, but now this outer skin was green with moss, bulging and sagging with the damp of many winters. The whole surface was an intricate map of cracks, some several inches wide, others as fine as hairs. Here and there large pieces had dropped off and revealed the rows of rose-pink bricks lying beneath like ribs. There was a whole landscape on this wall if you peered closely enough to see it; the roofs of a hundred tiny toadstools, red, yellow, and brown, showed in patches like villages on the damper portions; mountains of bottle-green moss grew in tuffets so symmetrical that they might have been planted and trimmed; forests of small ferns sprouted from cracks in the shady places, drooping languidly like little green fountains. The top of the wall was a desert land, too dry for anything except a few rust-red mosses to live in it, too hot for anything except sun-bathing by the dragon-flies. At the base of the wall grew a mass of plants, cyclamen, crocus, asphodel, thrusting their leaves among the piles of broken and chipped roof-tiles that lay there. This whole strip was guarded by a labyrinth of blackberry hung, in season, with fruit that was plump and juicy and black as ebony.

The inhabitants of the wall were a mixed lot, and they were divided into day and night workers, the hunters and the hunted. At night the hunters were the toads that lived among the brambles, and the geckos, pale, translucent with bulging eyes, that lived in the cracks higher up the wall. Their prey was the population of stupid, absent-minded crane-flies that zoomed and barged their way among the leaves; moths of all sizes and shapes, moths striped, tessellated, checked, spotted, and blotched, that fluttered in soft clouds along the withered plaster; the beetles, rotund and neatly clad as business men, hurrying with portly efficiency about their night's work. When the last glow-worm had dragged his frosty emerald lantern to bed over the hills of moss, and the sun rose, the wall was taken over by the next set of inhabitants. Here it was more difficult to differentiate between the prey and the predators, for everything seemed to feed indiscriminately off everything else. Thus the hunting wasps searched out caterpillars and spiders; the spiders hunted for flies; the dragonflies, big, brittle, and hunting-pink, fed off the spiders and the flies; and the swift, lithe, and multi-coloured wall lizards fed off everything.

But the shyest and most self-effacing of the wall community were the most dangerous; you hardly ever saw one, unless you looked for it, and yet there must have been several hundred living in the cracks of the wall. Slide a knife-blade carefully under a piece of the loose plaster and lever it gently away from the brick, and there, crouching beneath it, would be a little black scorpion an inch long, looking as though he were made out of polished chocolate. They were weird-looking things, with their flattened, oval bodies, their neat, crooked legs, the enormous crab-like claws, bulbous and neatly jointed as armour and the tail like a string of brown beads ending in a sting like a rose-thorn. The scorpion would lie there quite quietly as you examined him, only raising his tail in an almost apologetic gesture of warning if you breathed too hard on him. If you kept him in the sun too long he would simply turn his back on you and walk away, and then slide slowly but firmly under another section of plaster.

I grew very fond of these scorpions. I found them to be pleasant, unassuming creatures with, on the whole, the most charming habits. Provided you did nothing silly or clumsy (like putting your hand on one) the scorpions treated you with respect, their one desire being to get away and hide as quickly as possible.

Examination assignment

Question 1: Comparative Analysis

Read the following three texts. Compare the ways in which the writers use language to convey their feelings about the incident being described. You should concentrate on such matters as:

◆ purpose
◆ audience
◆ context.

Question 2: Evaluation of Analytical Methods

Using the three texts you have analysed in Question 1, highlight the ways in which you have interpreted these three texts and evaluate the approach to analysis you have used, saying which you have found the most useful in shaping your responses to the three texts.

Text A

An Edinburgh schoolboy tells of the gangland fights in Scotland's capital city. Adapted from *English Accents and Dialects.*

> Aw it's the gangs . . . they just fight with knives and bottles and big sticks . . . and bricks . . . takes place over at the big railway over there . . . they've got a gang . . . they call it Young Niddrie Terror . . . round here they call it Young Bingham Cumbie . . . and that's how it starts . . . they start fighting . . . and they fight with other yins, they fight with . . . Magdalene . . . that's away along the main road there . . . if . . . Magdalene's just down that road . . . and they fight with the Northfields . . . and they go away on buses . . . and go to a lot of other places . . . to fight . . . aw . . . about sixteen and that . . . there's only one person that lives round here . . . this part . . . and the rest are . . . some of them live away up the road there . . . and they're all round the scheme . . . well . . . there's one of them . . . he . . . he takes a lot of them on, he's right strong . . . well, they . . . they have nicknames . . . I forget his name but . . . his nickname but . . . he is strong . . . he fights with all these others . . . he takes about three on at a time . . . because he is big . . . aw, the police come rou . . . round just . . . just when it starts . . . see all the police at night, they're going round the scheme . . . making sure there's no fights . . . and all the laddies just run away when they see the police coming . . . aye . . . they run away and hide . . . till they think it's safe . . . they take them away down to the police station . . . well, if there's any serious . . . injuries on anybody . . . they'll get put in the children's home or that . . . so if they're old enough they'll get put there . . . Billy . . . he was caught . . . just a couple of nights or so ago . . . some of them . . . some . . . aw, they usually . . . there's wee-er laddies than me that goes round there and start tossing stones at the laddies round there. They usually get battered fae them if they get caught.

Text B

A killer goes to the house of one of his prospective victims in Iain Banks' novel, *Complicity.*

> You're already wearing your moustache and wig and glasses and you have clip-on sunshades over the lenses because it is quite a bright day. You ring the doorbell,

watching down the drive for any cars while you pull on your leather gloves. You're sweating and nervous and you know you're out on a limb here, you're in the process of taking some terrible risks and the luck, the *flow* that comes from being justified and in tune and not taking too much for granted, not being contemptuous or disrespectful of fate; all that's in danger here because you're pushing the envelope, you're maybe relying on one or two things going perfectly. Even getting it all set up to get you this far may have taxed your fortune to the limit already and there's still a long way to go. But if you're going to fail you'll do it full-face on, not flinching, not whining. You've done more than you thought you'd ever get away with and so in a sense it's all gain from here, in fact it's been all gain for some time and so you can't complain and you don't intend to if fate deserts you now.

He comes to the door just like that; no servants, no security phone, and that by itself gives you the green light; you haven't the time for any finessing so you just kick him in the balls and follow him inside as he collapses, foetal on the floor. You close the door, take off your glasses because your vision is so distorted, and kick him in the head; far too softly, then still not hard enough, as he scrabbles round on the floor, one hand at his crotch and the other at his head, making a spitting, wheezing noise. You kick him again.

This time he goes limp. You don't think you've killed him or severed his spine or anything but, if you have, that can't be helped. You make sure he can't he seen from the letter flap, which is covered by a sealed box, then you look round the hall. Golf umbrella. You take that. Still nobody coming. You walk quickly through, see the kitchen and go in there, pulling down the Venetian blinds. You find a bread knife but you keep the umbrella too. You find some tape in a kitchen drawer and go back to the front hall, turning him round so that you're between him and the door. You tie his hands and wrists together. He's wearing expensive-looking slacks and a silk shirt. Crocodile slip-ons and monogrammed socks. Manicure and a scent that you don't recognise. Hair looks slightly damp.

You take off both his shoes and stuff both socks into his mouth; they're silk, too, so they ball up very small. You tape his mouth closed, put the roll of tape in one pocket, then leave him there to search the rest of the house, pulling down the blinds in each room as you go.

Text C

This article by Ian Hislop is from *The Sunday Telegraph*, 22 June 1997.

It was one of those very hot days when bad temper seems to hang in the air. I got on the train into Victoria and found it crowded and sweaty. Sitting down without really looking where I was going, I discovered I was perched next to three black youths who were smoking.

They were not merely smoking but smoking in that deliberate, surly fashion that defies the conventional commuter to point out that it is a no-smoking carriage.

They smoked threateningly and stared sullenly at everyone in the carriage, only occasionally breaking into a mutual exchange of expletives. It suddenly really annoyed me that on what was a steamy, unpleasant journey I had to inhale their cigarette smoke as well. So I asked them politely to stop.

I am not puritanically anti-smoking, nor am I particularly keen to confront surly youths on trains, but occasionally one forgets what the world is like and thinks that it must be possible on an ordinary weekday morning to ask someone to observe the law without risking one's life. The youths, who must have been between 14 and 16, refused to stop. They seemed pleased that someone had risen to the challenge so that they could then display their contempt for them.

A number of other passengers asked the youths to stop smoking as well and they responded by becoming more abusive. One passenger, looking angry, walked over and again asked them to put their cigarettes out. They told him to sit down. He did not want to sit down. They told him to sit down more forcefully and he knocked the cigarette from the hand of the youth sitting nearest the aisle.

That was it. That was the trigger and within what seemed like a fraction of a second all three of the youths were on their feet laying into the man with their fists and kicking him. They had clearly done this sort of thing before and shouted to each other to 'smack him in the f***ing mouth'. The man went down and after a punch in the face his glasses went flying. The three of them continued to attack him until the other male passengers intervened. We tried to separate him and the youths with some success but the scrapping continued until I decided to pull the emergency cord. The train stopped suddenly and so did the fighting.

The youths regrouped at one end of the carriage muttering to themselves and the man sat down at the other end. 'Always got to be a f***ing hero,' shouted one of the youths as the middle-aged man, looking anything but heroic, tried to put his glasses back together. He did not seem to be injured and it looked as if no one had been hurt until we all noticed an elderly black woman who was wheezing and shouting at the youths. In their desire to beat up their fellow passenger they had kicked this poor woman out of the way, winding her badly.

'How dare you?' she kept screaming at them. 'How dare you!' There was then a silence while the train sat motionless. The silence seemed to go on a long time.

'He tried to burn my hand,' said one of the youths, presumably trying to think up some sort of defence. There was more silence and for some reason I felt guilty about pulling the cord and making everyone late for work. So I apologised to the carriage. One of the youths told me to 'shut [my] f***ing mouth'. The black woman shouted 'Hooligans' at them. We waited again.

Eventually, an official came along to the carriage looking very nervous indeed. He said nothing but took out a key and switched off the alarm that I had triggered. He did not ask who had pulled the cord or why they had pulled it. He simply turned the key and then, sweating profusely, left the carriage the way he had come. The black woman was outraged.

'I want the police to come,' she said, pointing at the youths. 'I want the police to come and beat their guts in.' I can't convey the force of her emotion, but those were exactly the words she used.

Student response

Analytical comparison

Although these three texts are linked through a general theme, of incidents of violence, their styles and individual viewpoints are notably different. The purposes of the three texts also vary from entertaining the reader in the novel, to informing the listener and reader respectively in the schoolboy's speech and the newspaper article.

The first text is spoken and this therefore affects the style of the language and the content. Broadly, the purpose of it is to inform the audience about fighting in Edinburgh, but we can also see that it has been used as part of a linguistics text. Consequently, in this latter context, the subject of the speech is less important than the way in which it is spoken. The audience for this particular text must therefore be the readers of the book, but originally it was an interviewer, face to face with the speaker.

There are several features of this text that denote it as speech and make it different from the other written texts. For example, there are many pauses and fillers showing the speech is spontaneous. The speech is very fragmented, perhaps because there may be questions from the other participant in the conversation. For example, there are no obvious connections between '. . . to fight . . . aw . . . about sixteen . . .' The fillers are used to allow the speaker thinking time before the next idea. Some information that the child is disclosing is also context bound to the situation. An exophoric reference such as 'there's only one person that lives round here,' can only be understood if we know where 'here,' in this instance clearly a place, actually is.

Because the mode of this text is spoken, there is little or no overt description; the information is comprised mostly of facts such as '. . . they just fight with knives and bottles and big sticks . . .' The only form of description around the facts are indications of size, for example, use of the adjective 'big' or 'wee-er'. The latter of these is of course an example of a comparative adjective from a specific dialect, which is significant considering this text is a dialect study.

The speaker is clearly separated from the incidents by the use of the third-person plural pronoun 'they' to refer to the hooligans. The use of non-standard forms of English, such as 'other yins', suggests that the situation is informal and the use of this dialectal noun indicates that he speaker is at ease. There is also a large amount of ellipsis and

→

contraction, such as 'it's' instead of 'it is'; this obviously helps to make real speech less laborious and more concise but also shows that the speaker has slipped into a conversational style, even though he is being interviewed.

Text B shows a clear contrast with the spoken extract. The principal difference must be the purpose of the piece. As an extract from a novel, its purpose is to entertain the reader. It must therefore be more descriptive and engaging than the spoken piece, which is merely to impart information to the listener. The novelist has a wider scope of methods to recount his story and information and this extract uses some particularly interesting techniques. Without the introduction for extract A, the topic of the speech may not be immediately apparent. However, the title of the novel, 'Complicity', gives an insight into the novel's content and theme of partnerships in crime. A further interesting feature is that it is written in the second-person narrative form, a very unusual voice for a novel, and usually more suited to instructional writing. This serves to involve readers and make them characters in the story, indeed making them *complicit* in the action. The reader is drawn into the narrative in lines such as '. . . if you're going to fail you'll do it full face on . . . You've done more than you thought you'd ever get away with . . .' This voice makes you a 'partner in crime' to the violence that is part of the text. This has the effect of heightening the violence. This contrasts to Text A where the second party, the listener, is so much more distanced from the content of the boy's speech.

The reader is also drawn in by the immediacy of the present tense: 'you tape his mouth closed.' These events give the impression of happening now. Verbs such as 'ring,' 'close,' and 'kick' are all active, creating a strong sense of action and involvement and make the act so much more immediate, unlike the reporting of the violence in Text A, which is distanced through the third-person voice and past tense.

Unlike the spoken mode, description is possible and almost necessary in a fictional work. It increases the interest and overall effect on the reader. Information can be given about the setting: '. . . no servants, no security phone and that by itself gives you the green light', as well as the protagonist's feelings: 'You're sweating and nervous . . .' Such information is rarely necessary or possible in spontaneous speech. The style also allows for the notice of small details such as the victim wearing a 'silk shirt', 'monogrammed socks', and being 'manicured'. All these details help to build up a more complete picture of the situation the reader is placed in, again heightening the participation. The text is graphic and specific: 'he scrabbles . . . making a spitting, wheezing noise.' This language is that of someone directly observing the action and its precision once more intensifies our part in the violent act.

→

The audience for text B is perhaps more general than that of text A. Novels are widely enjoyed. But the rather distasteful subject matter of this novel and the unusual style perhaps mark it out for an adult audience, with possible voyeuristic tendencies.

Text C could be described as a halfway point between texts A and B. It contains elements of both and also has certain features of its own genre. Because it is an article from a newspaper its purpose is mainly that of conveying information to its readership. It is not a main news story, so therefore it has more flexibility in the way it is written, yet it must remain clear and interesting. It is similar to text A in that its topic is a real incident of violence. However it is related in the form of a story. The small amount of speech in text C is quoted and the speaker marked. ' "He tried to burn my hand," said one of the youths . . .' Because there are several people involved in the story, it is necessary to identify who is speaking. The speech is also unambiguous; there are no pauses or repetitions, showing that this is not transcribed speech and has therefore been adjusted by the writer, so that it is easier for the audience to understand.

Although detailing a real incident, the piece is more descriptive than an eyewitness account, sharing some of the qualities of text B. There is a sense of setting and place. 'It was one of those very hot days when bad temper seems to hang in the air.' This sets up an atmosphere of menace through the simple adjectives 'hot' and 'bad'. The writer furthers this appeal to his readers by use of the carefully chosen parallel formation of the words 'merely' and 'surly'. Adjectives are also used to further describe feelings and place: the train is 'crowded and sweaty'. But the characters are also depicted in a way that affects the way we feel towards them. The description of the youths as 'surly' gives a forewarning of what may happen and emphasizes the tension. The elderly woman is clearly and rightly seen as the victim in the eyes of the writer, through the use of the simple adjective 'poor'.

The imparting of opinions is an important feature of this genre of writing, either directly or through insinuation. This feature does not occur in either of the other extracts. There is the potential for it in text A as it is a real-life account, but in text B opinions are not suitable, as we do not hear the author's own voice. The writer of text C expresses opinions about people. For instance, he suggests the uselessness of the train official by describing how: 'He said nothing . . . He did not ask who had pulled the cord . . . He . . . left the carriage the way he had come.' The simplicity of the information adds to the feeling of brevity over the length of time the official spends in the carriage.

The lexis that the writer uses gives clues as to the probable audience of this article. There are some fairly complex or unusual lexical choices, such

→

as 'perched' to describe sitting. The complexity of the language suggests an informed, educated audience, who also understand and feel with the opinions of the writer.

Like text A, the piece is written from a first-person point of view, as an eyewitness account. But the fact that it is written in the past tense distances both writer and reader from the events detailed in the article, contrary to the technique of using the present tense, employed in text B.

Although these three texts are occasionally linked by similarities in style, mode and, clearly, theme, they also show three distinct and clear genres. We see the fairly emotionless, plain speech of the transcript, the involving, entertaining style of the novel extract and the opinions and clarity of the newspaper article. All are connected through topic but made individual through style, purpose and audience.

Evaluation of analytical methods

I decided to use a very simple framework for my analytical comparison. Firstly, by concentrating on the difference between the actual modes, I feel that I have accentuated the broad differences between the texts: they have slightly different purposes and their audiences are also fairly unique and at times quite specialist. Consequently, the comparison revolves around the fact that I viewed Texts A and B as being intrinsically opposite in terms of audience and purpose, with Text C coming somewhere in between the two.

Specifically, I concentrated on the purpose of Text A by highlighting some of the features that make it so obviously a spoken text. Features such as non-verbal characteristics, reference and dialect forms allowed me to underscore the spontaneity of the mode and allowed a valid comparative angle with the other texts. In terms of Mode Theory, this text is at one end of Leech, Deuchar and Hogenraad's continuum where conversational speech is the most spontaneous of forms and a printed book is the least spontaneous. I suppose that I could have also concentrated on matters such as formality when adopting such a mode comparison, although there appeared to be such an abundance of matters to discuss that this would have detracted from the detail of what I wanted to analyse.

I also chose to examine some of the non-standard and contracted forms in my analysis; this gave me another angle to focus on, which would provide a fruitful area of comparative analysis, since it allowed me to focus on the feelings of the speakers or writers. As a result of this I focused upon the voice of the speaker in Text A, on the fact of him being young, relatively simplistic in his sentence formations and fairly at ease with his audience. This contrasts to the second-person narrative voice of Text B where the writer seeks to implicate the reader in his crimes while using quite an educated voice to convey his thoughts. I also considered

→

using the evidence of the title of the novel as a way into my analysis of the narrative voice. This enabled me to scrutinize the tense as well as the adjectival use of the piece; these proved to be fruitful areas of analysis of the protagonist's feelings and gave a clear contrast to the voice of the young boy in Text A. The examination of such areas allowed me to focus much more explicitly on the violence of the text, and thus show the difference between the two texts, in terms of both purpose and audience.

When tackling Text C, which is aimed at an educated audience, there were a number of matters that I could deliberate over: the overt use of the writer's own voice through such matters as the way he emphasizes his opinions by adjectival and adverbial use. I also concentrated on the way that this text is so much more realistic than either of the other two texts, because of the immediacy of the subject matter and the fact that it is something within the audience's own experience. The other two texts are less realistic because of the extreme nature of the content.

While there were many ways I could have chosen to undertake this comparison, I feel that my choice of a simple comparison through an examination of audience and purpose has yielded an interesting analysis of each text, through examination of linguistic content and features. ◆

Examiner's comments

This is a straightforward response that shows how easy it is to construct an analytical comparison around three quite diverse texts. By emphasizing mode differences, the comparison takes on a linguistic angle that allows a commonality of comparison; it is also helped by the student's knowledge of mode theory, although this is not as firmly embedded in the answer as it might be. However, there are many positive points to reward here: the integrated but systematic analysis; the use of terminology in a very unselfconscious manner; the use of clear and carefully chosen examples to illustrate the points made; and the overview of audience and purpose. The candidate could have spent more time evaluating the effect of the texts more overtly, but this is a minor omission.

The examination of analytical methods demonstrates that a logical route through the texts can give a close and accurate reading of each text. There is sound reflection on the structure of the answer and the student details some of her methodology quite well. More could have been made of the way she focused on audience and purpose; there is also little reference to alternative methods of analysis, although this is hinted at in her reference to mode theory. This is a sound answer, but it would benefit from closer reference to her own textual analysis and the terms of her framework for comparison.